KIDS, MONEY & VALUES

KIDS, MONEY & VALUES

PATRICIA SCHIFF ESTESS AND IRVING BAROCAS

BETTERWAY BOOKS
CINCINNATI, OHIO

Kids, Money and Values. Copyright © 1994 by Patricia Schiff Estess and Irving Barocas. Printed and bound in the United States of America. All rights reserved. No part of this book may be reproduced in any form or by any electronic or mechanical means including information storage and retrieval systems without permission in writing from the publisher, except by a reviewer, who may quote brief passages in a review. Published by Betterway Books, an imprint of F&W Publications, Inc., 1507 Dana Avenue, Cincinnati, Ohio, 45207. 1-800-289-0963. First edition.

97 96 95 5 4 3 2

Library of Congress Cataloging in Publication Data

Estess, Patricia Schiff.
Kids, money and values / by Patricia Schiff Estess and Irving Barocas.—1st ed.
p. cm.
Includes bibliographical references and index.
ISBN 1-55870-333-0
1. Saving and thrift. 2. Finance, Personal. 3. Children's allowances. I. Barocas, Irving. II. Title.
HQ784.S4E77 1994
332.024—dc20 93-33800
CIP
AC

Edited by Donna K. Collingwood
Interior design by Sandy Conopeotis
Cover design by Brian Roeth
Chapter opening illustrations by Ursula Roma

Betterway Books are available at special discounts for sales promotions, premiums and fund-raising use. Special editions or book excerpts can also be created to specification. For details contact: Special Sales Director, Betterway Books, 1507 Dana Avenue, Cincinnati, Ohio 45207.

With ever-lasting love to my teachers:

My parents, Adele and Milton Schiff, who made parenting look so easy.

My children, Andrea, Peter and Jennifer Wohl, and stepson, Noah Estess, who proved it was not.

Pat Estess

To my wife, Ellen, who has always lovingly supported me in all my endeavors and my children, Caryn and Ed, who live by those human values I cherish most.

Irving Barocas

ABOUT THE AUTHORS

Patricia Schiff Estess, author of *Remarriage and Your Money* (Little, Brown & Co.), has written extensively on families, values and money in national magazines, among them *Parents*, *Working Mother*, *Parade* and *Entrepreneur*. Now the president of Working Families Inc. and publisher of the *Working Families* newsletter, Pat concentrates on helping parents manage the tug of war between work and family, something she knows about firsthand since she was the editor of *Sylvia Porter's Personal Finance Magazine* at the same time she and her husband were raising four children.

Irving Barocas, an elementary school educator of thirty-seven years, is currently principal of General Studies at the Yeshivah of Flatbush Elementary School in Brooklyn, a position he has held for the past eight years. He has also been a public school administrator in Long Island and New Jersey for seventeen years. He has had a particular expertise and interest in the teaching of mathematics and has trained both parents and teachers in this field. During much of his professional career, he negotiated contracts for both teaching and administrative organizations.

ACKNOWLEDGMENTS

When you want good ideas about parenting, you go to the source—parents in the throes of the adventure and those who have survived it and are pleased with the kids they've raised. You also talk to kids to find out what's on their minds. To all those who have shared their stories, thoughts and ideas with us (and there were many), we give our profound thanks.

Some people deserve special recognition. Judy Rosenbloom, longtime friend and master teacher, introduced us to the girls, boys and teachers at Lawrence Middle School in Lawrence, New York, and let us share ideas in group settings with over a hundred youngsters who told us what they thought about money, values and parental guidance.

Over fifty girls and boys of the New Jersey "Y" camps (Cedar Lake and Nah-Jee-Wah) told us what value they place on the various occupations in society and how they reached those conclusions.

Howard Bramson and his fifth-grade class at the Yeshivah of Flatbush helped us refine and develop some of the activities in the book. So did art teacher Carol Levine and school librarian Rivy Abramson.

Many years ago Lois Rosenthal and Pat Estess spent much time thinking and writing about kids, values and money management. Their early work was the genesis of this book.

Editors are important in a subtle way. They keep books on track and authors on deadline. Ours did both—intelligently and sensitively. Thank you to Mark Garvey and Donna Collingwood.

On a personal level, there are people who provide authors with support and encouragement. We never stop being grateful for our respective spouses, Gene Estess and Ellen Barocas, who play that role in our lives.

Pat Estess and Irving Barocas

Chapter One

Parenting

Passing on Our Values

Kids are never home-free just because they've left home.

Look into a crowd. Can you distinguish parents from people who don't have children? No. After all, we parents look similar to normal folks. It's what rests on our shoulders that makes us different. Not our brows, but our minds furrow with concern because we know the early years will have a dramatic impact on how our children grow up and what they will consider valuable in their lives.

How am I going to teach Jessie that money doesn't grow on trees?

How I am going to say "no" to the Nintendo game set when Noah knows we can afford it?

Should I pay Mark for raking the leaves or expect that just because he's a member of this family he should assume that responsibility?

I don't know whether to get Anne a new bike to replace the one that rusted because she kept forgetting to put it into the garage or teach her a lesson and let her stay home, bikeless, when her friends are out riding.

Three challenges confront us.

The first: How do we launch our kids into the next millennium with values we are proud of?

The second: How do we rear these children so they can also adjust to an ever-changing world and to a society that isn't the same as it was when we were growing up and one that will hardly be recognizable (to us or to them) twenty years from now?

The third: How do we act as models for them—not just as people who endlessly moralize or criticize? (And that's a scary thought, especially because they're looking to us for answers we don't necessarily have.)

Values, those principles that guide a person's decisions long after he or she has left childhood, can be taught. And money can be used as a teaching tool, because money is a tangible part of a child's life.

At age two, Karen giggles with glee as she drops a fistful of coins into a hat-shaped porcelain toy and hears them clink.

At age three, Peter looks forward to shopping with his babysitter so that he can "pay" the cashier.

At age six, Eddie spends three-quarters of an hour shopping for the right $1.25 birthday card for his dad.

At age eight, Andrea balks at being able to use only half the $25 she gets as a birthday present from her grandparents; the rest of it has been "put away" by her mother, but she doesn't know where.

At age ten, Jen has to decide whether to go bowling or go skating over the weekend; she doesn't have money from her allowance for both.

As children grow, so does their involvement with money. Dr. James U. McNeal, a professor of marketing at Texas A&M University, recently surveyed fourteen hundred families about how children spend money. What he found was that they have a lot of it to spend. The average weekly income of children from their allowances and payments for household chores increased dramatically—by 73 percent—from 1989 to 1991. For five-year olds, the jump was to $5 a week, up from $2. Among preteens, weekly incomes topped $8 from allowances, gifts from grandparents, and "workfare"—payments for performing chores. In August 1992 alone, Dr. McNeal reports that kids age four to twelve will spend an estimated $1 billion of their own money on back-to-school purchases that their parents don't or won't cover, such as expensive shoes and jeans.

Yet statistics reveal that an astounding number of young adults have no real understanding of money-management principles—those skills that foster independence and a sense of responsibility. Nor does it seem that young adults have a clear picture of how money relates to values or principles.

This book is written for parents with children in those formative preschool through preteen years, parents who want to help their children develop skills and values, and parents who want to get involved with their children. It is written for parents who want to do the "right" thing, but sometimes aren't sure what the right thing is. And it is written for parents (grandparents, relatives, childcare providers or friends) who think guiding children in the direction of responsible adulthood can be fun. (That's one of our values: Learning is fun.)

If you have comments or activities that you'd like to share with the authors, please write to us at Betterway Books, F&W Publications, Inc., 1507 Dana Avenue, Cincinnati, Ohio 45207.

HOW DOES YOUR CHILD GROW?

The chart on pages four through nine defines the stages children go through when it comes to money, possessions and ethical values. The ages given are approximate and should be thought of as a guide to the stages of development. What's listed as a six-year-old characteristic might reflect where your six-year-old is—or it may not. Yours might have passed that stage at five or may not reach it until seven. Don't be alarmed! These are just approximate ages. (Material adapted from the writings and research of Arnold Gesell, M.D., Frances L. Ilg, M.D., and Louise Bates Ames, Ph.D.)

WHAT KIND OF FUTURE DO YOU SEE FOR YOUR KIDS?

In what seems like a blink of the proverbial eye, we find ourselves standing on the front steps waving a confused, perhaps emotional good-bye to a child who is embarking on a life uniquely her own. And we wonder what will become of her. Will she have what it takes to meet life's challenges?

To understand how to rear this future adult, we have to understand what type of person we want this child to become. Once we determine that, we have a clearer idea of how to model ourselves and how to help this child reach adulthood with the moral values and money-management skills we think are important.

The questions in the parent quiz on pages ten through thirteen have no right or wrong answers, but they help clarify what's important to each of us and what we want our children to value.

Look ahead. When your child is a young adult and ready to make these decisions, how would you want him or her to act in each of the following situations? On a scale of 1 to 5, circle the number that most nearly reflects where you fall between the two statements that appear for each question.

Age	Arithmetic Skills	Interest in Money, Spending and Saving	Personal Property	Honesty and Truthfulness
5	Counts by ones to ten or twenty—sometimes "skips" a number. Some can do addition and subtraction on fingers. Usually can recognize pennies and perhaps other coins (nickels, dimes, etc).	Interest in money is not strong. May like to give storekeepers coins in exchange for items.	Little trouble about possessions—doesn't seem to want more than they have. Shows pride in possessions but doesn't take good care of them.	Tells fanciful stories and exaggerates, but is beginning to distinguish real from make-believe and usually knows when he is "fooling."
5½	Can count to twenty. Writes numbers to ten with some reversals (Ɛ for "3" for example). Adds and subtracts correctly within five with fingers or in mind. Can name penny, nickel and dime.	Money only important for what it will buy—"money for candy" age. Little or no sense of saving. Will linger at counter, picking up and handling objects before buying.	Likes to have many possessions. May start "collecting" certain types of toys, odds and ends, etc. Very poor at taking care of things (may even like to break things). Strong feeling of possessiveness.	May "take" things they really want such as toys from friends or candy from a store. Less exaggeration and untruth-fulness—usually distinguishes fact from fancy.

Age	Arithmetic Skills	Interest in Money, Spending and Saving	Personal Property	Honesty and Truthfulness
6	Counts to thirty or more. Counts by ten to ninety or one hundred. Counts by fives to about fifty. Names coins and knows how many pennies are in a nickel or a dime. Writes numbers to ten or twenty. Adds within ten; subtracts within five. Likes to group objects by their properties—all round things together, all red things togeter.	Money interest is still in terms of what it will buy. Careless with money—loses it. Spends immediately and thoughtlessly. Still no sense of saving. Many children get allowances by this stage.	Likes to take things to school to show and share; takes school work home to show parents. Still irresponsible, with possessions—loses them, breaks them and scatters them around the house. Bargains or barters. Poor sense of value and will often make a poor trade. Miscellaneous collecting and accumulating.	Needs are strong and sense of ownership weak—may take property of others. Conversely may give away private possessions. Can't bear to lose—may cheat at games. Falsehoods often told to avoid blame. Some very honest verbally at this stage, but will still cheat at games.
7	Counts to one hundred by ones, fives and tens. Can name all coins and knows how many pennies are in each. Can add sums to twenty or more. Can subtract from ten.	Increasing interest in money. Most want an allowance. Some earn extra money by doing "extra" chores. Beginning interest in saving for a future purchase.	More interested in possessions and takes better care of them. A greal deal of collecting. Bartering—mostly an "even swap." May give away own things.	Less taking of possessions of others but may take items of little value, such as school pencils, erasers or small, inexpensive such as attractive items like mother's cosmetics or jewelry.

Age	Arithmetic Skills	Interest in Money, Spending and Saving	Personal Property	Honesty and Truthfulness
8	Begins counting by groups such as threes and fours. Knows addition and subtraction facts by heart. Adds and subtracts three-digit numbers with borrowing and carrying. Can do simple multiplication and division.	Interest in money and relative value of coins. Begins to be "money mad"—loves to acquire money; likes to "earn" money; knows how much they have, what they want to buy and what it will cost. Plans ahead as to what they will buy. Saves up for expensive items—little squandering of money for trivial things (except for trendy items such as trading cards or comic books). Getting good at bartering and trading.	Great interest in property and possessions. Likes to acquire, own and barter objects. May hoard, arrange and gloat over possessions. Want a place of their own to keep things. Some take good care of things, but most still tend to be careless. Room and clothes tend to be untidy but will keep some things neat that are important to them. Likes to bring things to school that are related to school topics. Not very aware of real estate as property of others. Will take "short cuts" across property and may even cause damage.	Children feel they "need" what they "want." If not provided, may "take" money that is now meaningful for what it will buy. May take household money to "treat" friends. May tell tall tales and boast. Knows fact from fancy and may size up adult to see if the adult believes stories.

Age	Arithmetic Skills	Interest in Money, Spending and Saving	Personal Property	Honesty and Truthfulness
9	Knows the "times table" through nines. Can divide by one-digit numbers. Learning to use fractions and measurements. Can keep simple accounts and records.	Likes to have large amount of money to count, look at, show and talk about. Less interest in allowance; may even forget to ask for it, but will ask for money when they want something. Can do "extra chores" for money but not always interested enough to do so. Buy some of their own supplies (crayons, comics, etc.) and will ask for money to buy them. Interested in cost of different items. Can save up small sums to get a more costly item.	Begins to be neater. Does not lose things as easily as before. Some effort at cleaing up room (usually after parent reminder) but still may not hang up clothes. Particular about own possessions and may consider them and her room "sacred." Still very much into trading and bartering. May spend much time classifying and cataloging collections and possessions.	Ethical standards are set; may be very exacting of self and others. Very few at this stage deliberately take things not belonging to them. If forbidden to do something like reading comic books, may do so secretly. Most can lose in competitive games fairly gracefully. More truthful at this stage. Some exceptions: May exaggerate or say they've washed hands when they haven't; may support a friend or sibling in a lie.

Age	Arithmetic Skills	Interest in Money, Spending and Saving	Personal Property	Honesty and Truthfulness
10-11	Proficient in most whole number operations. Beginning to understand relationship of decimals to fractions. Interested in applying skills rather than merely acquiring them. Can solve many problems involving money.	Needs are greater and may need frequent adjustments in allowance. Can plan and save for larger expenditures. Likes to earn "extra" money—chores, outside "jobs," starting a "kid's business." Can set up a simple weekly budget.	Good sense of personal property and usually takes care of things, though girls are usually neater and more organized. Does not want parent to enter room unannounced or to "touch" property. May be compulsive in organizing possessions or collections. Usually respects others' property, but still may "trespass" by walking through lawns, etc.	Usually good, law-abiding citizen at this stage. Understands need for rules and regulations. *But,* great variations at this stage. "Normal" child is not always uniformly "good." Sometimes selfish, deceitful or destructive. At this stage children are interested in the moral dilemmas of their times—the environment, treatment of old citizens, homelessness, etc.

Age	Arithmetic Skills	Interest in Money, Spending and Saving	Personal Property	Honesty and Truthfulness
12-14	Can do all operations with whole numbers, fractions and decimals. Begins to understand ratio, percentage. Capable of understanding and figuring profit and loss, interest on savings, etc.	Needs are greater. So is interest in money. Likes to shop and "hang out" at malls—more interest in clothing by both sexes (but more by girls). Boys tend to have greater interest in electronic gadgets. Again, a need to review spending and allowance. At this stage, may want more than they really need. Conflict arises with parents over spending habits. Still can save for more expensive items but have conflicts over what is wanted now versus what is wanted through patient saving.	Great variation on care of personal property. Some neat and organized; others sloppy. Very possessive about own property within family but may lend easily to friends. While possesive of own things may borrow Mom's blouse or Dad's sweater without permission.	Great variation in honesty. Much depends on sense of trust established within family in earlier years. If good sense of trust, little tendency for dishonesty or lying, despite being in "rebellious" stage. Usually, lying will center around behavior they know parents would disapprove of. Or will lie to protect a friend. Peer pressure is great at this stage—may engage in dishonest acts such as shoplifting because friends are doing it.

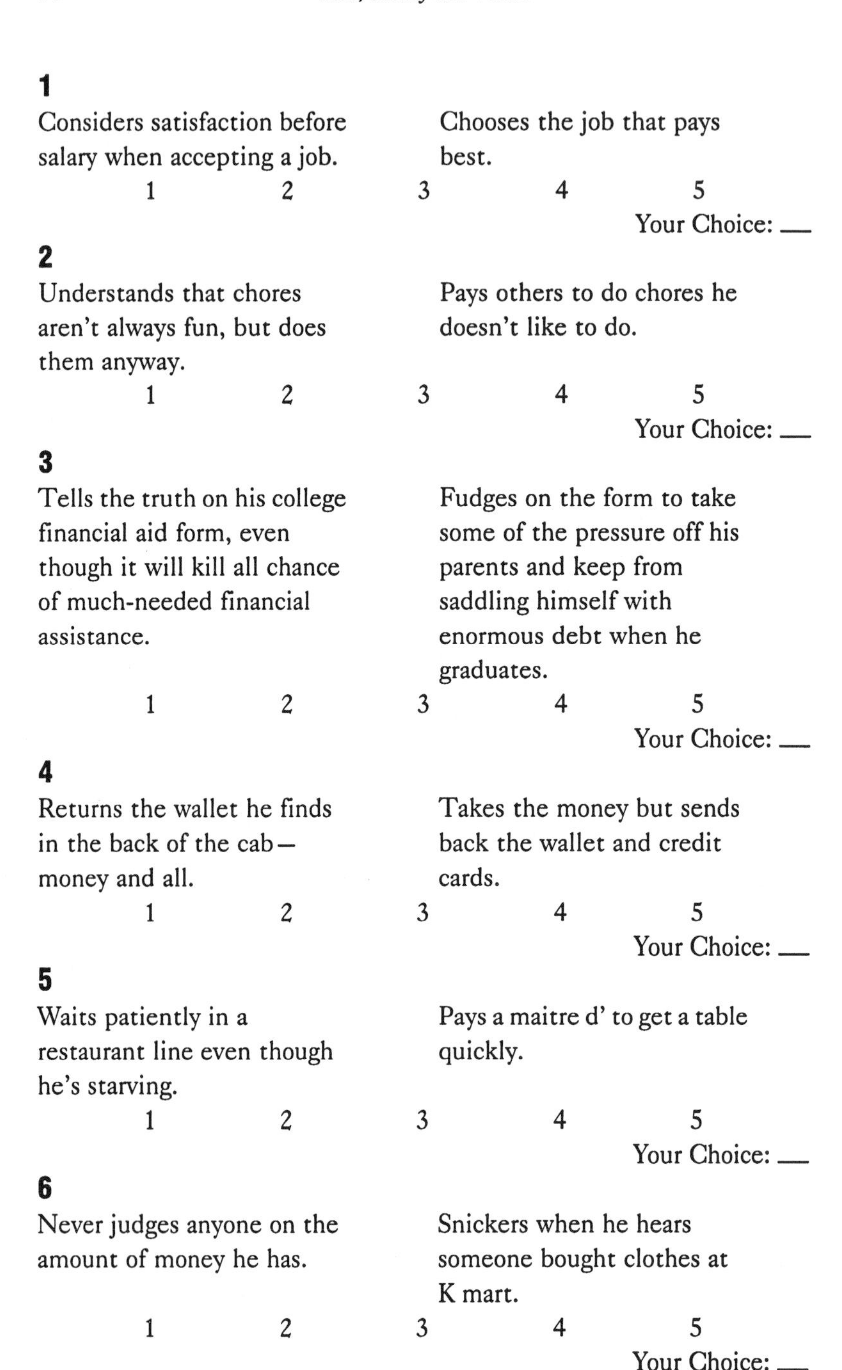

1

Considers satisfaction before salary when accepting a job.

Chooses the job that pays best.

1 2 3 4 5

Your Choice: ___

2

Understands that chores aren't always fun, but does them anyway.

Pays others to do chores he doesn't like to do.

1 2 3 4 5

Your Choice: ___

3

Tells the truth on his college financial aid form, even though it will kill all chance of much-needed financial assistance.

Fudges on the form to take some of the pressure off his parents and keep from saddling himself with enormous debt when he graduates.

1 2 3 4 5

Your Choice: ___

4

Returns the wallet he finds in the back of the cab—money and all.

Takes the money but sends back the wallet and credit cards.

1 2 3 4 5

Your Choice: ___

5

Waits patiently in a restaurant line even though he's starving.

Pays a maitre d' to get a table quickly.

1 2 3 4 5

Your Choice: ___

6

Never judges anyone on the amount of money he has.

Snickers when he hears someone bought clothes at K mart.

1 2 3 4 5

Your Choice: ___

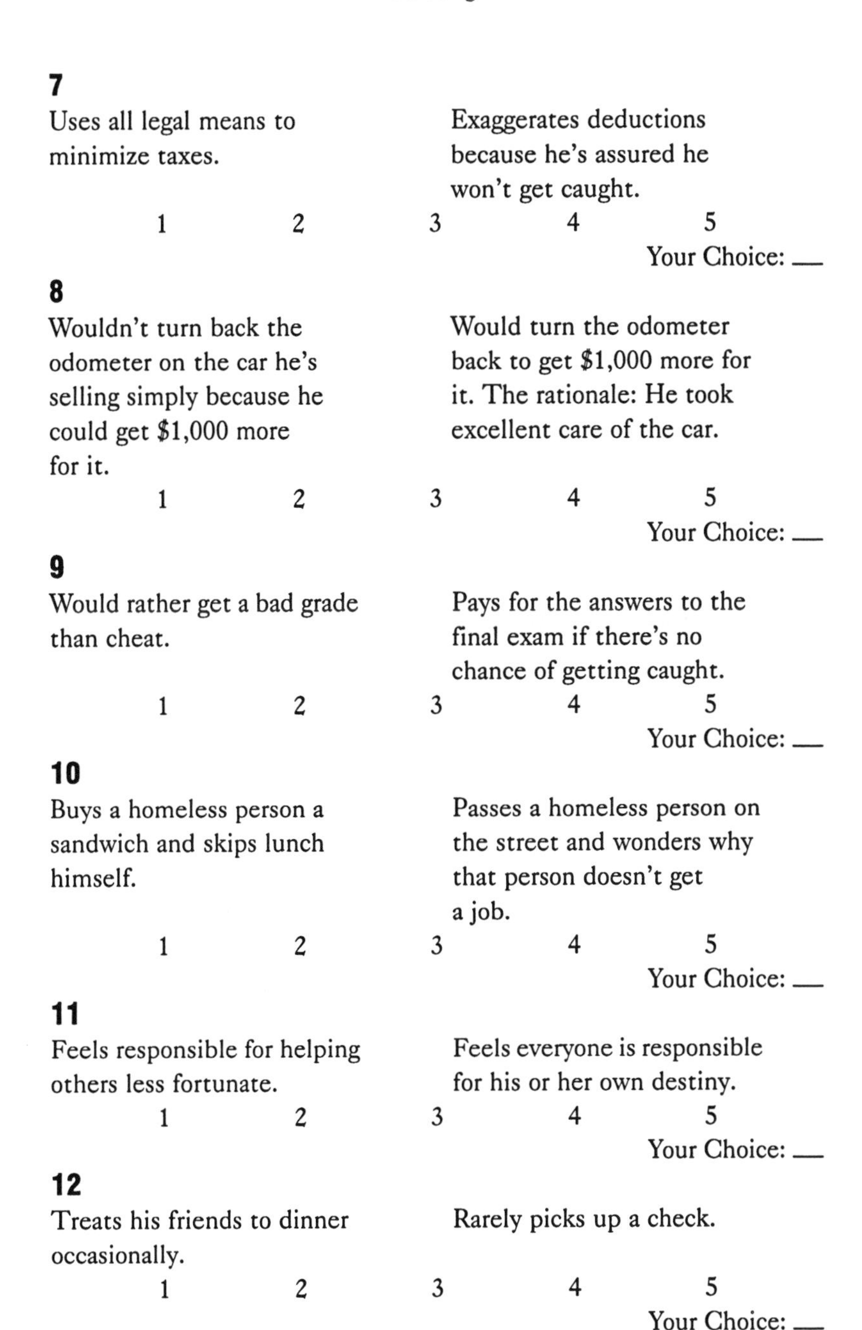

7

Uses all legal means to minimize taxes.

Exaggerates deductions because he's assured he won't get caught.

1 2 3 4 5

Your Choice: ___

8

Wouldn't turn back the odometer on the car he's selling simply because he could get $1,000 more for it.

Would turn the odometer back to get $1,000 more for it. The rationale: He took excellent care of the car.

1 2 3 4 5

Your Choice: ___

9

Would rather get a bad grade than cheat.

Pays for the answers to the final exam if there's no chance of getting caught.

1 2 3 4 5

Your Choice: ___

10

Buys a homeless person a sandwich and skips lunch himself.

Passes a homeless person on the street and wonders why that person doesn't get a job.

1 2 3 4 5

Your Choice: ___

11

Feels responsible for helping others less fortunate.

Feels everyone is responsible for his or her own destiny.

1 2 3 4 5

Your Choice: ___

12

Treats his friends to dinner occasionally.

Rarely picks up a check.

1 2 3 4 5

Your Choice: ___

13

Pays off each credit card's monthly balance completely.			Has a number of cards, each with a residual balance.	
1	2	3	4	5

Your Choice: ___

14

Saves for the future.			Thinks you're only young once—he'll save when he gets older.	
1	2	3	4	5

Your Choice: ___

15

Buys himself what he wants or needs, if he can afford it.			Hesitates to buy something because he's afraid to spend money.	
1	2	3	4	5

Your Choice: ___

16

Balances his checkbook monthly.			Sees no need to balance a checkbook; the bank will do it.	
1	2	3	4	5

Your Choice: ___

17

Is ingenious about finding ways to earn money.			Doesn't work if she can't get the job she wants.	
1	2	3	4	5

Your Choice: ___

18

Understands his personal finances.			Has no interest in personal finance.	
1	2	3	4	5

Your Choice: ___

19

Prides himself on using his own money to buy a car.			Asks you for money for a new car instead of using his own.	
1	2	3	4	5

Your Choice: ___

20

Arranges for his own rides or uses public transportation when his car is being repaired.				Borrows your car when his is in the shop.
1	2	3	4	5

Your Choice: __

Add your scores on questions 1 through 9.

A score of 21 or less means you are probably more values-oriented than acquisitions-oriented. If your score is higher than 22, the reverse is probably true; material possessions play an important part of your life. Values and acquisitions are not necessarily in conflict. But values-oriented people will usually be guided by a strong sense of ethics and acquisitions-oriented people will usually be guided by what brings them immediate gratification.

Moral and ethical decisions, when in conflict with something that will make life easier, nicer or more comfortable, are not always easy. In fact, as these questions illustrate, these decisions are often downright difficult and painful to make. But the values we instill in our children when they are young will serve them well when they are adults—for they guide people's actions as parents, spouses, employees and employers, community members, relatives and friends. And they pilot you through the stormy days as well as the bright ones.

Add your scores on questions 10 through 12.

A score of 7 or less indicates you're a person who cares deeply for others, one who is willing to make personal sacrifices to ensure the well-being of others in addition to your own. In all probability, you are rearing your children that way. If your score is over 8, you're probably rearing children who will be more concerned with themselves than others.

Add your scores on questions 13 through 18.

If your scores total 14 or less, your aim is to see your children grow into financially responsible people. If your score tops 15, you may not be giving enough thought to whether your children are interested in or adept at managing their personal finances.

Add your scores on questions 19 and 20.

With total scores of 5 or less, chances are your children will have developed financial independence when they leave home. Scores of more than 6 mean you need more emphasis on helping your children build self-esteem and competence so that they can leave your home and feel confident they can make it on their own.

A LAMP UNTO OUR CHILDREN

Children learn from watching grown-ups they respect—most often their parents. If we are lured into buying a new car because this year's model out-dazzles the one we're driving, why wouldn't our children ask for the latest video game even if they got the one they wanted last year? If we walk into a store for a pair of shoes and wind up with six, why should our children not follow in our footsteps? If we complain about money (or lack of it), fight about it with mates, get lazy about managing it, go on spending binges, we can count on our kids to do the same (or, in a few cases, to be the opposite because they're rejecting us as role models).

So not only do we have to supervise our children's growing up, we also have to monitor our own actions. This parenting is quite a responsibility!

Could it be that children become the light of our lives because we, as parents, have to be a lamp unto them?

Chapter Two

While They're Still Tots

What Preschoolers Can Learn About Values

Scene: Day-care facility when mom comes to pick up three-year-old Jonathan.

Mom: How's my little guy doing?

Day-care worker: Well, we're having a little trouble. Jonathan still won't share toys, food or anything else with the other children and he often grabs things away from them.

Your Choice of Responses

You can:

1. Spank him every time you get a report like this.
2. Tell him he has to change and as encouragement give him a dime every time he shares.
3. Praise him every time he shares. Return anything he grabs from others and explain that things cannot be taken without permission.
4. Let him see you sharing with others, including with him. And let him see you politely ask others to share with you.

A LOOK BEHIND THE RESPONSES

Choices (1) and (2) just don't do the job at all. Three-year-olds are simply too "me" and "mine" oriented. They're just learning to socialize. Hitting a child just signals that hitting is acceptable when you're displeased and can only lead to even more aggressive and unacceptable behavior toward others. Bribing a child with a dime teaches that behaving properly is only done if there's a material reward attached. Taken to an extreme, you can see this bribery setting the stage for a teenager holding a door for an elderly person only if he gets paid for it!

Steadily and consistently practicing choices (3) and (4) should help a child learn about sharing—but it won't happen overnight. Praising appropriate behavior and showing how to redirect inappropriate behavior (such as giving back the truck after Jonathan has snatched it from his friend Amy and saying firmly but kindly to Jonathan, "We don't take things without asking.") is helpful.

Even more helpful is to smile broadly, hug him and say "thank you" when he shares something with you. "Me" oriented toddlers want to please a parent.

A PRESCHOOLERS' UNDERSTANDING OF MONEY

"Not *my* child" we say to ourselves when our friend, near hysteria, tells us about her eighteen-year-old son who ran up a $1,500 credit card bill in his first three months at college. "I'm going to start early teaching *my* Kelly about money," we think as we look down into the stroller and watch Kelly play with her stuffed animal.

With that in mind, we race to the bank with Kelly to open a savings account, telling her en route how important it is to save for the future. And when we get home we begin teaching Kelly to count coins so she will learn the value of money.

As seemingly logical as those actions are, they don't lay the foundation for good money management skills for Kelly . . . or for any preschooler.

Preschoolers have little understanding of money. Most of them think we get money from the lady in the grocery store or that, like a magician's string of colored scarves, it exists in a never-ending supply in their parents' pockets.

Nor do they understand savings. If you have any doubt about the strength of their interest in the here and now or their disinterest in the future, just ask a three-year-old to hang onto her candy from midday until after supper. Even if there's a further enticement, such as "if you can wait to eat it until then, I'll let you stay up later to watch your favorite TV show," chances are the candy will not make it through the midafternoon *Sesame Street* program.

As for the connection between counting money and its value, it doesn't exist. Children under age five may be able to count. They can count the six dollars on the table and then they can count the six people in the room. But without putting a dollar in front of each person, most are unable to understand that each of the six people could get a dollar bill. They need to *see* the connection before they can conceptualize it. To prove this to yourself, try the following exercise with a member of the under-five set. Place five pennies in each of two rows as pictured below.

Ask the child to count the pennies in each row. Then ask which row has more. In most cases, despite counting five in each row, the child will point to the bottom row because the "spread" of the bottom row makes it appear greater to the young child.

If teaching values and savings are beyond the developmental abilities of preschoolers, what's a parent to do about establishing good money habits and attitudes early on in a child's life?

INSTILLING VALUES THROUGH INFORMAL LEARNING SITUATIONS

Concentrate on a well-balanced, sensible approach to seemingly nonmoney related areas, such as feeding and toilet training. Psychologists see a strong connection between babies who are immediately rewarded with feeding when they aggressively grab for the bottle or breast and adults who must have what they want when they want it—they are highly competitive people in their dealings with money. Psychologists also see a strong connection between children who are rigidly toilet trained (made to sit on the potty for long periods of time after every meal, for example) and miserliness or the unwillingness to spend or give up something of value. Parents must be aware that our responses to infant and toddler activities that are unrelated to money management sometimes convey attitudes such as instant gratification and rigidity that stretch into adulthood and are manifested in money-management behavior.

What is a sensible approach to feeding? Demand feeding—providing a bottle or breast when the infant is hungry—has pretty much replaced the more rigid approach that advocated feeding by the clock every four hours or so. But what is appropriate for an infant is not necessarily appropriate for a toddler, because as children grow, they are more capable of controlling and postponing urges. If parents satisfy a toddler's every need and respond to each urge, we wind up rearing a self-centered youngster. So it's incumbent on us to help a child delay feeding gratification and learn patience. As the child grows, these skills will be transferable to other aspects of life.

What's a sensible approach to bowel training?

Don't start too early. While children's readiness to "go on the potty" varies widely, most aren't ready to approach this task until fifteen or eighteen months of age (others not for many more months). Until then, they can't control their sphincter muscles enough or even give the signal that they need to use the bathroom.

Attract the child's attention to the start of a bowel movement. To do that we have to give the act a name—something your family is comfortable with. Just by saying, "Ralph is having a B.M.," we accomplish three important goals: showing the child we're interested in what he's doing, making him aware of what he's doing and giving him a word he can use to tell us what he wants to do.

Since the child now knows this act interests us, he usually gives a signal that he is about to have a movement. When he does, it's time to establish a connection between having a movement and the place to have it. Suggest he sit on the potty, even if it's too late. He gets to associate the act with the potty. One day the B.M. and sitting on the potty will coincide.

Take children shopping with you. As chaotic and aggravating as it can sometimes be, shopping with children is a wonderful learning experience for them. Though toddlers are too young to understand the value of money, they begin to see that those pieces of green paper and shiny round metal objects given to a storekeeper "buy" something in return. It's the beginning of an awareness that money is a medium of exchange. Let the child be part of the exchange by handing the storekeeper a dollar for the newspaper and allowing the child to receive the paper and the change. Eliminate crankiness by making the shopping trips short or breaking up longer ones with playground stops.

Don't mistake love for money. We're living in a time when many parents are away from their children for long stretches—either because they work eight or more hours a day or because they are divorced and don't live with their children. Guilt about the time apart has parents dipping into their pockets and coming up with money or gifts as substitutes for time missed or as a way of saying "I love you," causing the child to associate feelings of love with "things."

Presents, of course, are expressions of affection, but they're not substitutes. The hugs, time together and general warmth between parent and child provide the basis for an emotionally healthy child and that emotional health translates into healthy attitudes toward money and possessions later in life.

Understand that you're a role model. Our actions and reactions will be mimicked by our infants and toddlers, because they see us not as we really are but as the wisest, most knowing people in the world. What we do must be right!

A person with a living room that's off-limits to the family and only inhabited when company is visiting is sending the message that company is more important than family. Far wiser is to plan a less formal, more comfortable room when children are small and change it over to a more decorous room gradually when they are older and can care for and appreciate expensive furnishings. Simple rules, such as using a coaster under a glass or picking up and putting away toys after they've been played with, can be instituted at a young age.

A parent who screams about the accidental breakage of an expensive decorative plate indicates that "things are more important than people." To prevent that message from coming across, treat children as you would treat a guest. If a guest broke the dish accidentally, we would first ask if the person was injured or if any glass got into the skin. Then we would say, "Don't worry. Accidents happen." For toddlers and preschoolers, accidents are a way of life.

A parent who leaves compact disks lying around may be sending a message that a child could interpret, years later, as "it's all right to be careless with money." If a parent wants to teach a child responsibility and organization, it's best done by example. And just as this parent needs a CD holder, so do children need places for their possessions.

These psychological interpretations to early childhood training are not meant to leave parents confused, nervous, guilt-ridden or worried about how today's actions will affect a child's attitudes about money in years to come. As world-renowned baby doctor Dr. Benjamin Spock said, "Don't be afraid to trust your own common sense."

ACTIVITIES

Shopping Smarts

The supermarket may be routine drudgery for you, but to a preschooler it's an adventure. Here are a few ways to capitalize on the excitement and teach some valuable skills:

- Encourage your child to count potatoes, onions, oranges and other produce as she puts it in the plastic bag.
- While in the produce department, talk about the different sizes, shapes and colors of the same fruit (for example, all pears don't look alike) and the different weights and sizes of fruit. The large hanging scale gives you a chance to show a child the difference in weight between ten grapes and ten grapefruits.

- While still in the produce department, talk about what goes into making your selections — for example, why you're choosing the firmer apple over the softer one.
- Give a child a dollar to buy a nutritious snack (and talk about what "nutritious" means beforehand). Let her pay for the snack herself, get a receipt, hold the purchase in her own paper bag and keep the few coins in change from the transaction.

Knowledge From the Kitchen

Another miraculous learning lab is the kitchen. Try some of these skill-building activities:

- Let your child put away clean flatware in the drawer. Children love matching things and enjoy sorting the large and small spoons and forks and placing them correctly in the dividers.
- Let older preschoolers help you count how many people will be eating and how many plates and glasses will be needed to set the table.
- Talk about pouring a fourth of the milk in the quart container into a glass, about cutting an apple into thirds, or about sharing your sandwich by dividing it in half. You are "talking fractions" and doing it in a literal way children can understand.
- Cook or bake with children. Think of what goes into the simple act of making brownies: First, you have to decide which size bowl will be big enough to hold the batter. Then, you have to measure the ingredients and follow instructions as to what goes in first, second and so on. Then you have to decide which size pan you will need for baking the brownies. Then you have to set the timer and not forget to take the brownies out of the oven. All of this develops a foundation for sequencing and measuring, among other skills.

Penny Toss

Give your tot four pennies and have the child try to throw the pennies into a bucket or pail placed a few feet away. As he does, ask the following questions and count out the answers together (the rudiments of addition): "How many pennies are in the bucket?" "How many pennies are outside the bucket?" "How many pennies altogether?"

As he gets more adept, you can vary the questioning to familiarize him with the concepts of subtraction. "How many pennies did you start with?" "How many did you get in the bucket?" "How many are left outside the bucket?"

After a while, try to get the child to predict what will happen even before he tosses the coin. "If you start with four pennies and three go into the pail, how many will have missed?" Increase the number of pennies in the penny toss as he gets more proficient.

Counting Relatives

"How many cousins do you have?" can be the start of a relative counting game. The child names them and you write them down and together you count the names. You can keep adding categories (aunts, uncles, friends) and then combine them. "How many aunts and uncles do you have?" (The same approach can be used with other items, such as categories of clothes—socks, shoes, red shirts, blue jeans, etc.)

Chapter Three

Allowances

To Give or Not to Give

Scene: Living room. Parents look up from reading the newspaper because nine-year-old Allison is speaking.

Allison: "Can I get an advance on my allowance? I bought a set of felt-tipped pens because I need them to make my social studies project look great, so I don't have anything left for the movies.

Your Choice of Responses

You can:

1. Show your understanding by digging into your wallet and giving her enough to cover a movie and popcorn.
2. Grumble about how you're always having to bail her out as you dig into your wallet and advance her enough to cover a movie and popcorn (knowing it will never be paid back).
3. Suggest to Allison that this is the time to review how much she gets for an allowance. Perhaps it's not enough.
4. Hand her the *TV Guide* and suggest she look through it because she won't be going to the movies with her friends.

A LOOK BEHIND THE RESPONSES

If, on occasion, you ante up the money and charge it as an advance (1), you're not doing anything horrible. (Haven't we all gone over budget or borrowed from a checking plus account at one time or another?) But if your child finds herself in this position often, something is wrong and digging into your pocket to make her solvent again isn't the answer. Better to sit down with her to find out why (3). Is she mismanaging her money? Is the amount she's getting insufficient for her needs? Are her wants too grandiose?

Having her stay home (4) is appropriate if, after the allowance review, you discovered your child was not managing money well. In that case, you might have to replace the feeling of guilt over ruining a child's plans with a feeling of responsibility: You're a responsible parent helping a child understand the consequences of her actions. (There comes a time, after all, when parents must indicate that they are not a never-ending source of funds.)

Grumbling when handing out money (2) is definitely a mistake because it causes resentment and anger and doesn't teach anything about money management or values.

WHY ALLOWANCES?

"Why allowances?" some parents ask. "Whenever Dan wants money, all he has to do is ask. We usually give it to him."

We think of allowances as having two reasons for being:

1. So children can learn to manage money.
2. So children can share in the family's resources.

Can't Learn to Manage What You Don't Have

Who makes decisions about what to do with money if children ask a parent for money every time they need it? The parent, of course. But if children have money of their own to spend or save, they have to make the decisions and choices—even if those choices are on a small scale.

Think of it this way. For a child, managing money that's not his is like riding a two-wheeler while someone is running beside him balancing the bike. He will stay upright because of your guiding hand. But because he won't be allowed to balance the bike himself, he'll never go very far or become an expert rider. (Allow)ances (allow) children to practice making little mistakes with a little money in the hope that someday they won't make big mistakes with a lot of money.

A Child's Share of the Family's Resources

A weekly allowance provides children with spending money—but it does more than that. It reinforces the idea that as a member of a family, a child is entitled to a designated portion of the family's resources.

If that's the case, do you withhold an allowance because a child hasn't folded her laundry or set the table as she was asked to do?

Do you withhold an allowance because she didn't do her homework or wouldn't try succotash?

Do you withhold an allowance because she carelessly lost last week's allowance, slugged her brother when he was bothering her or stuffed a fistful of M&Ms into her mouth right before dinner?

Do you increase the amount you give her because she was nice to the neighbor or got an A on a test?

No. To all these questions.

We feel strongly about keeping an allowance separate from chores, love, approval, punishment and reward.

The allowance-chore connection. Sammy hadn't set the table because he went over to Adam's to play and didn't come home until dinner was on the table. His older sister Martha was assigned his task in his absence and did it begrudgingly. And we, as parents, are angry too. We've come home tired and still have to prepare the family dinner. We expect some help; setting the table is a perfect chore for Sammy at this age. And, we wonder not too silently, what kind of irresponsible child we are rearing.

If Sammy's punishment is a reduction in his allowance (or no allowance at all next week because this was the third time in the last six days he "forgot"), the underlying connection is that he can "get away" with not setting the table—by paying for it.

This doesn't teach the *value* you want him to understand: *Responsibility goes along with being a family member.* Just as withholding the allowance doesn't help teach responsibility, neither does it suppress a parent's level of frustration with not having the chores done. One mother tells this story about linking allowance to chores. "I had told her that for every chore she didn't do that she was supposed to do, I'd deduct one dollar from her allowance. Each week I'd deduct more money. One day after walking from room to room observing what she hadn't done, I blew my stack. My daughter looked at me as if I were crazy. 'Listen,' she said, 'I'm not really interested in money, so why should I do the chores?' "

So how do you teach a sense of family responsibility that later in life will expand into a sense of societal responsibility?

Capitalize on a child's natural sense of industry. Children like to help out. They like being praised, hugged and congratulated for doing a good job. They like having a sense that they belong to a family that works together.

Nevertheless, there are times when their sense of responsibility is dwarfed by their forgetfulness or their itch to get out of doing something. Certainly, you can't let chores go unnoticed or undone. So you may have to prod or redirect behavior. Here are but a few of the ways Sammy could be brought into the fold:

1. Insist that Sammy take over Martha's job of clearing the table and rinsing the dishes. If rinsing dishes is too difficult for five-year-old Sammy, then clearing the table for the next two nights might make Sammy understand that he is not going to get out of helping out.

2. Call Sammy a half hour before dinner to tell him to come home or buy him a watch, teach him to tell time, and make him responsible for being home at the appropriate hour.

3. Sammy can set the table before he goes to Adam's house.

4. In addition, you, as the parent, and Sammy can reexamine the table-setting chore. Is it something that *he* has to do, or can he do something else that will be helpful for the family, something he wouldn't forget? If he's going to be visiting friends four out of

six nights and will not be home to set the table when you want it set, perhaps he and Martha could switch permanently, since she's always in a big hurry to get on the phone with her friends after dinner. Or perhaps he could have the job to regularly fold the laundry after supper.

Tip: If possible, try to give children a say in which chores they do. Some, like straightening a room or hanging up wet towels in the bathroom, are mandatory. Others, such as raking leaves, washing the car or emptying the dishwasher, can be negotiated according to availability, talents, age and likes—especially if there is more than one child in the family and the kids can work out an equitable split.

Tip: Find chores that challenge children instead of always piling on the tasks we don't like to do. Doling out dull jobs teaches the exact opposite of what we want our children to learn. We make work seem like unpleasant duty, but we want to demonstrate that it can be challenging and fun. Certainly, menial tasks must be done, and those can be shared. At the same time, though, give every child a chance to take on something more exciting, such as cooking a family dinner, reorganizing the kitchen cabinets, shopping at the supermarket, or planning a sibling's birthday party.

The allowance-school work connection. What value would be reinforced by withholding an allowance because homework wasn't finished—or even started? Are homework, education and learning important to you? If so, children should not be allowed to buy their way out of it by giving up part or all of their allowance.

STICK-TO-ITIVENESS CHART

Although attention spans vary by task and by individual, this developmental rule of thumb chart might help you in figuring out appropriate tasks:

One Minute of Total Concentration for Each Year.

Concentration Time: three minutes = three-year-old
five minutes = five-year-old
eight minutes = eight-year-old
ten minutes = ten-year-old

So how do you emphasize values *and* make certain the child's homework is done?

Monkey see, monkey do. Set aside a quiet work time for the whole family to do "homework." You can use the time for any number of things, some of which you like to do and some of which you have to do, such as paying bills, catching up on correspondence or reading.

Indicate that homework is an important and serious endeavor. You can do that by (1) making certain children have all the necessary supplies for homework, (2) providing a place they feel comfortable working in, (3) listening to their problems so they know they have your *support* for their endeavors (not necessarily your help) and (4) helping them remember their responsibilities, perhaps by posting on the refrigerator a monthly calendar, which has large daily boxes to allow each child in the family a place to fill in what he or she is supposed to do for school the next day.

Should children be told in advance that they will be rewarded with money (or things) for doing well in school? Absolutely not.

If you bribe children (and that's what you're doing) to do well scholastically, you take away their pride in achievement and play to their greed. You also set up a frustrating and unfair system in your home if you reward the bright child who skims by, doing as little as possible to get *A*s, and don't reward the child of average or below average intelligence who works hard to get *B*s, *C*s or *D*s. So what can you do to indicate to children that their efforts are valued?

Tip: Unexpected and special treats, such as picnics or "stay up late Friday nights," are nice rewards for children who have put *a lot of effort* into their schoolwork. With them, you're saying that the energy they put into schoolwork has a value all its own. But don't promise anything in advance or you put yourself in the briber's position again. And don't get into the routine of always coming up with a treat after the child has done well. In his excellent book *Parenting by Heart*, Dr. Ron Taffel tells why: "Behaviors are quickly given up if they're rewarded *every time* they happen. As soon as one or two rewards are skipped, the learned behavior diminishes or stops," he says. But "if the frequency and timing of a reward varies—sometimes you get one, sometimes you don't—the learned behavior *persists*." Translated: A great report card can and should, every so often, net some nonmaterial reward, such as special time together, a favorite dinner, a relaxation of the homework rules once in a while or asking the child if he can help you add up the numbers in your checkbook. (After all, there's no more powerful reward than someone feeling needed.)

The allowance-love connection. If you subscribe to the philosophy that an allowance should be seen as a money-management tool and as the child's share of the family's resources, you see immediately there isn't an allowance-love connection. But inadvertently falling into the habit of connecting money and love is easy: "I love you, so I'm giving you more allowance." It's fraught with danger, however. If your child buys into it, you face a number of possibilities. He could assume that money can also be used to buy love or friendships, and he could begin buying friends gifts all the time or constantly treating them to activities. He could learn to measure love using money as the yardstick in his relationships. So if, for example, you have to cut back on his allowance (because the family is going through difficult financial times), he assumes you don't love him.

These, of course, are not the messages you want to send.

HOW MUCH IS THE RIGHT AMOUNT?

Figuring out how much allowance to give children provides a prime opportunity to sit down together and talk about values and principles involved in managing money.

No matter what a child's age—six or sixteen—certain elements go into the determination of what's appropriate.

Family values: Do parents want children to learn the value of saving and charity? If so, is money for either or both to come out of the allowance?

Amount of money available: The family's income and its obligations to other family members must be considered.

What is included in the allowance: Is lunch money covered? Clothes? Transportation? Guitar lessons? After-school snacks?

Age of child: The older the child, the more needs must be covered.

The "going" rate for children of that age in the community: The comparison can be made with a child whose family has values similar to yours and an allowance that covers the same items. Does your child get "extras" that her friend has to pay for out of an allowance?

ALLOWANCE TIPS

Start an allowance when a child starts elementary school. School signals the beginning of important responsibility for a child.

Set a specific time when money is distributed and stick to it. Being late with an allowance leads children to wonder whether parents can be counted on and implies that it's OK to be irresponsible.

Distribute allowance at the beginning or in the middle of the week. Like adults, children spend most of their money on weekends. Giving them their allowance early in the week forces them to think about how they'll spend it later and teaches them to wait for what they want.

Make it large enough so that some of it can be saved. If a kindergartner gets $1 a week and every penny is accounted for, you lose the "planning ahead and saving" component of money management.

As children get older, increase their allowance and what their allowance covers. This gives them more experience managing larger sums of money and more opportunity to make choices.

Taking on More Responsibility—A Clothing Allowance

Clothing allowances are becoming increasingly popular for older children . . . and for good reasons. They want more of a say in what they wear. They use clothes as a means of expressing their individuality or of conforming with their friends. And they simply don't appreciate their parents imposing adult taste on them.

Parents like it too. Those working full time don't relish the thought of a Saturday shopping spree with their adolescents (which usually winds up as a growling match). Reasons of parental sanity aside, a clothing allowance helps older children learn to manage larger sums of money. Parents marvel at the tight-fistedness youngsters develop when they have to spend their own money. All of a sudden, they notice that items children swore they "couldn't live without" when the parent was paying, are getting a second look or being thought of, suddenly, as "not that important."

After you've determined how much money you spend on the child's clothes each year, there are several ways you can structure a clothing allowance. Here are two examples:

1. Divide the annual amount into four parts: one for each season. If the annual amount comes to $1,200, that's $300 per season. (Winter clothes cost most because of coats and boots, so share that information with youngsters. They have to recognize that some budgeting will be necessary to see them through the fall and winter seasons.)

2. Dole out money monthly in twelve equal installments. This requires a youngster to do more planning than the seasonal distribution because money will have to be carried over from month to month for big purchases.

Negotiating Allowance Raises

Children's "cost of living" expenses increase at what seems like a geometric rate as they move from ages eight to eighteen. As a responsible adult, you have to acknowledge that and, wherever possible, make provisions for it. More money can certainly be earned as children grow (and we'll talk about earning possibilities in a later chapter). But should an increase in an allowance be in order, teaching kids to negotiate that hike is a valuable money-management lesson.

Whether a raise is in order at the time, it makes sense for you to initiate a discussion about money on a yearly basis—perhaps on the child's birthday. Or, if there is some new development in the interim that requires a second look at the amount, encourage your child to bring up the subject.

Asking for a raise is an ideal time for kids to learn the fine art of negotiation.

Let's run through one oft-heard conversation.

Scene: Mom, rushing to get ready for work, is fending off a request for a raise from her nine-year-old:

Mom: I just raised your allowance three months ago. When is it going to be enough?

Daughter: It was too little to begin with and it's still not enough. I get $10 a week and most of my friends get $15. Sally Barger gets $20.

Mom: Sally's father is a doctor and can afford more. Besides, I think her parents spoil her. She gets too much money for a kid her age.

Daughter: I get nothing. Not even things I need.

Mom: I have no time to discuss this. You just don't know how to manage money. Stop spending on foolish things.

Retake.
Same scene.

Mom: I would like to talk about the raise you asked for, but I just don't have the time now. Suppose we set aside an hour after dinner, say next Thursday night, to talk about this. That will give both of us time to get a few things together. I want to think about our finances in general and how much money we have for allowances. And you need to put together a list of what you've spent over the past week. Will you also find out what Sandy Cooper gets for an allowance and what her allowance covers? And finally, if we find you do need more money, will you think of other ways that you could get it in addition to or instead of raising your allowance.

With the second response, Mom makes several important points:

1. She indicates this is an important subject, one that warrants more discussion than the time it takes to brush her hair and hunt for her coat and pocketbook. She asks to set aside a quiet, appropriate time.
2. She insists her daughter take the responsibility of providing some objective criteria by which to determine whether a raise is in order.
3. She indicates that Sandy Cooper's family has values corresponding more closely to hers than any of the daughter's other friends.
4. She gives herself time to review her own finances, since she can only allocate what is available to her.
5. She urges her daughter to think of ways other than increasing allowance to get more spending money.
6. She has framed the discussion in a nonthreatening, responsible way and has taken the personal accusations out of the dialogue.

MISTAKES KIDS MAKE WITH ALLOWANCES

If there is one of us who hasn't made most of the following mistakes at least once (more likely, many times), let that person stand in the hall of incredible boredom, for childhood should be a wonderful, safe place to err. So despite the nuggets of money-management wisdom we impart to them on a regular basis (which they just as regularly ignore!), we can expect nothing less than a passel of mistakes from our children. As parents, our role is to structure our criticism so that it's gentle enough to nourish growth without destroying the still weak roots of confidence that have been set down.

Mistake #1: The Week Is Longer Than the Allowance

Overspending is a disease of sophisticated governments and people of all ages. So don't be shocked or worried if your child winds up with no money a few days before his next allowance.

How to handle this: Only you know the answer to the question of whether the child's overspending is a chronic problem or something very unusual. If it's chronic, you'll want to take immediate action *by doing nothing*. Bailing out a child who constantly overspends sends the wrong messages: (1) You'll always be there and (2) it's okay to be irresponsible about money. If, because of not having any money, the child threatens to skip lunch (figuring, rightly, that you'll never agree to let that happen), accompany him to the kitchen and *show him* (don't do it) how easy it is to make a sandwich and pack a piece of fruit.

Whether the problem is chronic or occasional, find out how destitution came about. Ask him to recap his expenditures that week. Ask him how he thinks he could have handled it differently. (You're planting the "savings seeds.") But you're not unreasonable either. If the situation was a strange one that couldn't be helped and his needs for money are dire, it's no sin to advance him part of next week's allowance. But reserve this "advance" technique for the desperate times or your child will become deft at the "buy now, pay later" school of economics.

Mistake #2: Your Child Makes It a Habit of Losing Her Allowance

How to handle this: Again, the key question is whether this is a frequent or a rare occurrence. Even if it happens once a year, it may signal that the child is disorganized or simply naïve about how easily money can fall out of pockets, pocketbooks or books.

Find out where the child is keeping his money. If it's squashed into the back pocket of his pants, suggest he neaten it out and keep it in his front pants pocket (where it's easier to spot a dollar that's slipping out). Sometimes kids put their money in books or pocketbooks that they leave somewhere or lose. Getting your children fanny packs to strap to their waists can be a real boon.

Another suggestion you can elicit . . . or make yourself: "Don't take all your money with you when you go out. That way if you lose the money you have with you, you won't be flat broke."

Mistake #3: Your Child Lends Money to a Friend Who Doesn't Pay It Back

How to handle this: You don't want to teach your child never to lend someone money because there are times when all of us want to lend money to family or friends. But you do want to teach your child how to assess each request. Again, draw out the circumstances surrounding this loan and do so with gentle prodding questions: "Has Johnny borrowed money from you or other children before. . . and has he repaid it?" (This helps your child understand that a loan has to be made to someone reliable.)

"Wasn't Johnny the boy who tripped you last week? Was that an accident or does he do that to you often?" (This helps your child understand that he doesn't have to be bullied into something, that if he is going to lend money to a friend, it should be someone he likes and respects—and vice versa.)

"When did Johnny say he'd give you back the money?" (This helps a child understand that a loan is an agreement in which *both* parties have certain responsibilities.)

Mistake #4: Your Child Becomes an Incredible Cheapskate With Money—to the Point of Not Having Lunch So He Can Stash It Away

How to handle this: Overconcern and overmanagement of money leads to extreme frugality—one of the toughest problems among children. If you see it happening, recheck the allowance package. Is it a realistic amount for a child his age? Are your spending rules too stringent? If those aren't the situations, urge by example. Make it a point of telling him how much you're enjoying the new sweater you bought for yourself or how much fun it was to buy a birthday present for Aunt Edith. If the problem is severe and you find your child hoarding money saved by skipping lunch or some other extreme action, seek psychological help because the frugality might indicate a deeper emotional problem. (More about this in the chapter nine: Big Problems for Small Folks.)

ACTIVITIES

Weekly Job Rotation Chart

If the children in the family are capable of doing similar chores and they all moan over the same jobs, consider a weekly rotation chart using two different sized paper plates and a paper fastener. Draw it and write instructions next to it.

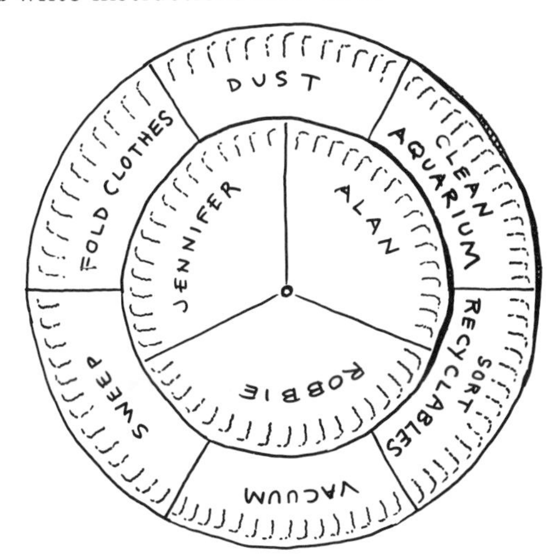

Allowance Worksheet

Use this chart when determining how much a child needs and what is to be paid for out of the allowance.

WHAT ALLOWANCE WILL INCLUDE

	Daily Cost	Weekly Cost
Lunches	__________	__________
Snacks	__________	__________
Transportation	__________	__________
Gifts	__________	__________
Contributions	__________	__________
Activities with friends	__________	__________
Buying personal things	__________	__________
Special to me (piano lessons, visiting friends across town)	__________	__________
Savings	__________	__________

Chapter Four

Spending

Helping Kids Outgrow the "I Want What I Want When I Want It" Syndrome

Scene: Main Street, U.S.A.—Passing a store window display of a new Game Boy cartridge "On Sale for Only $60."

Eight-year-old Anthony as he jumps up and down: "Oh, I need this cartridge. Timmy has it and it's great. This would only be my third cartridge. All the other kids have more. Please, Mom. Please, please."

Your Choice of Responses

You can:

1. Argue until the child sulks or cries.
2. Call in reinforcements: "I'm sick of your always asking for things. Wait until I tell your father."
3. Put off conflict by promising the cartridge for his birthday.
4. Launch into a ten-minute diatribe about money not growing on trees.
5. Give in and save yourself an argument.

A LOOK BEHIND THE RESPONSES

None of the choices is appropriate. If you argue until the child sulks or cries (1), you'll wind up with a whining, sulking kid who may get the idea that this type of behavior will get him what he wants. Calling for "father" (2) teaches the child that you are not a decision-maker and cannot be counted on to discuss important matters. Delaying a decision (3) can be a good tactic, but not by promising something you might have really not wanted to give the child. Launching into a lengthy discussion of money (4) is about as effective for your child as it was when your parent did the same to you many years ago. And capitulating to save yourself an argument (5) paves the way for a child to make greater and greater demands that he knows you'll cave into sooner or later.

Instead, the decision to buy the cartridge should be delayed so that you can review the following factors:

1. Can you afford it?
2. Is the game something you want your child to have?
3. Is it important that your decision be influenced by what other kids have?
4. Is your child making too many demands or are his requests reasonable—in number and in price?
5. Is this request a "want" or a "need"?

THE PSYCHOLOGY OF CHILDREN'S SPENDING

Long before they understand the concepts of saving, investing or borrowing, children sense the power of spending money. They see their parents show off purchases, ogle over a neighbor's new car, fight over a credit card bill or get teary-eyed when they receive presents of their dreams. They sense more subtle messages too—

the difference in a parent's response to them when they use their allowance for grandma's birthday present as opposed to six packs of bubble gum.

Bombarded With "Buy" Messages

The average six- to eleven-year-old watches twenty-three hours of television weekly and teenagers watch even more, say those who track such statistics. Conservatively that translates into at least two hundred commercials a week. Children face a temptation blitz.

Beyond dolls, toys, foods and gobs of sugarcoated cereals, manufacturers are selling kids security, self-image, popularity and status among peers. All of this is nothing new in the scheme of advertising: Weren't we after championship when we ate Wheaties, or glamour when we played with Barbie, or power when we rode skateboards? Other than the fact that the "toys" are different, has the advertising pitch changed that much now that we're adults? (More on advertising and consumerism in chapter seven.)

Needs or Wants: The Great Kid Dilemma

Only the phrase "I don't want to" outranks "I need" in frequency in children's speech. In some way, we adults are just big kids too. We mistake *want* for *need* on occasion, convincing ourselves that the newest album from our favorite musician is a need when indeed it might simply be a want. Because this need/want perception is tricky even for us, it's no wonder that children have trouble with it.

Start early in helping children differentiate between needs and wants. Much of their ability to handle their finances, now and later, depends upon knowing the difference. Spending on wants is wonderful, fun, interesting and important, but part of our responsibility as parents is to teach children that needs must be met first.

Listen to yourself. Are you using the right word? Are you using *need* for things that will provide you with necessities—food, clothing, shelter, good health and the ability to work? Are you using *want* for things you'd like to have, things to make you feel comfortable and happy? Do you need or want the wrench? Do you need or want the hard candy? Do you need or want the best-selling novel? Needless to say, it depends on who you are as to whether the wrench is just another piece of equipment or a necessary element of a tool box, whether the hard candy is necessary for your blood sugar level or whether it's just something nice to suck on, or whether the novel is just another good book or whether it is required reading for a course in American literature.

How you use *want* and *need* sends a message to your children about your value system. The only time the message runs afoul is when parents haven't thought through their own values and they send mixed messages to kids. Telling a son that he doesn't need another toy, after having bought yourself a bevy of "needed" electronic gadgets that are collecting dust after having been "played with" once, sends a mixed message.

Explain to children that people have different wants and needs simply because they live in different places, are different sexes or ages, or are physically or emotionally different.

Play the "Want It-Need It" game as you ride in a car, walk down a street or simply flip through the pages of a magazine together. Or play it in a more formalized fashion as it is set up at the end of this section. The child's answers provide you with a springboard to explain the concept more thoroughly.

"See that baby? Does she need someone to take care of her? Or does she want it?"

"Do you think you need toothpaste when you brush your teeth? Or do you use it because you like the taste?"

As children grow older and their worlds expand, the concept of needs and wants expands, as does the realization that needs are not the same for everyone. Yet, as kids feel pressure to conform to their peers, the distinction between needs and wants blurs.

Making Choices: The Second Great Kid Dilemma

Children make choices with money early in life simply because the supply of money available to them is limited. Even before they have money of their own, they are asked whether they want frozen yogurt or pretzels for a snack. Without realizing it, they are making a decision that will have consequences: By choosing the frozen yogurt today, they won't be munching on pretzels. That is the logical consequence of the yogurt decision.

Making wise spending choices requires complex, abstract reasoning powers that develop slowly through experience. It takes time for a youngster to realize that if she spends all her money today on things that look good, she will have nothing left to spend on things that look good tomorrow. But if children are to learn how to make wise choices, they must be allowed to make seemingly poor choices and live with the consequences without fear of ridicule. Money choices become even more complicated when you factor in the two other important and frequently used (and misused) assets people have—their time and their energy.

Kids Are Savvy Players

As if by some natural sixth sense, children know how to "play" their parents. They know which parent is the "toughy" and which is the "soft touch." They know when a "no" is a "no" and when it is a "maybe." And they know how hard to press for a "yes."

As parents, we are less intuitive about how to handle all the requests that are flying, mainly because we may have five or six going on at any given time and don't concentrate on how we're answering or what messages we're sending out. Distracted, we'll often mutter "we'll see" in response to a buying request, not realizing that this stalling tactic teaches nothing but procrastination. If we thought about it, we'd realize that a more useful and honest response would be: "Susan, I can't even think of that now. Please ask me about it when less is happening." With this comment, we're not committing ourselves (as we seem to be doing with "we'll see"), and we're teaching the lesson that important spending decisions require more than a reflexive response. They require thought and analysis. Too, it's important to examine whether the decision being made reflects our present monetary situation or the values we hold close. Are we saying "yes" to a request because we think the purchase is necessary or meaningful *and* we have the money? Are we saying "yes" for a future purchase because we approve of the request but just don't have the money for it now? Are we saying "no" because the purchase isn't needed, meaningful or important, or because there is no way we can ever afford it?

Don't hesitate to explain your rationale honestly. Saying you can't afford something instead of saying you don't think something is an appropriate purchase may put a halt to the requests for a while. But it's dishonest, confuses the family's financial picture in a child's mind, and sidesteps a parent's responsibility to teach values.

Information to Share With Children

In quiet moments, discuss with your children appropriate ways of requesting something. Share with them tips and information that will help them deal with you—and with others—in the future.

1. When the best time is to discuss purchases.

2. How you'd like to be approached, such as having them ask you the question, "When would be a good time to ask you about taking piano lessons?"

3. Why it's important to limit the number of times you ask for something. How it's more effective to ask for something once or twice than to nag. As soon as you equate it to your own repetitive requests to them, like "clean your room" or "do your homework," they'll understand how irritating and unproductive nagging can be. (And, of course, if *you* are nagging, the best tip of all is to find more effective ways of asking your children to do things.)

4. How your budget limits what you can afford to spend. Encourage your child to make compromises or consider different options for getting what he wants, such as saving his allowance money, waiting for the item to go on sale, buying a similar but less expensive model or doing extra household chores for pay.

5. From time to time a child will not understand your reasons for saying "no." Frequently that happens when your "no" is rooted in values, such as not wanting your child to have one more stuffed animal because enough is enough. Draw up a list of items you absolutely forbid in the house (perhaps because the advertisements for them are so offensive or because they violate your religious or ethical codes) and give it to the children. This lets them know beyond a shadow of a doubt not to ask for them. Explain that no matter what the price or how many times they ask, you'll just say "no." To you, these things are off-limits.

6. There will be times when you'd like to buy them something they want, but just you can't afford it. If this is the case, such as agreeing with them that having a computer would be wonderful, explain to them that you'll work with them to develop a savings plan for that purchase. Encourage creative options, such as matching the funds they've earned and saved for the computer or suggesting that they canvas local businesses, asking if the businesses are selling old PCs and, if so, would they sell or give away the old computers.

Learning From Themselves

Years of experience are needed to find the right balance between frittering away money on useless items and never enjoying a purchase because every cent is frugally stashed into savings. Many mistakes will be made along the way. That's the way it should be. To paraphrase James Barrie, God gave us memory so that we might handle money better in adulthood than we did in childhood.

Don't expect too much insight too soon when it comes to kids and spending. They may take years to learn how to distinguish between wants and needs and to make wise choices. (And even when they are officially "adults," they don't always get it right!)

ACTIVITIES
Dilemmas

This game leads children through the thinking process that goes into decision making and provides a basis for a talk about actions and consequences.

Create a set of "scenario cards" on 3″ × 5″ index cards, depicting everyday situations. Let your child pick one and discuss what the person in the situation should do next. Here are some sample situations:

1. Harvey goes to a record store with his friend and his friend's mom. He has $2.60 with him. He sees a tape of his favorite group on sale for only $3.20. What should he do?
2. Bob wants a pet dog. One of the kids at school is offering free puppies, but they're going fast. He asks his parents for one. They say, "Not right now." What should he do?
3. Sarah and Maria go to a bookstore to buy their own copies of a book their teacher read to them. When they get there, the bookstore has only one copy. What should they do?

All of these dilemmas have several acceptable (and some unacceptable) responses.

In the first situation, unacceptable responses would be to steal the tape, steal the money to buy the tape or lie to his friend's mom ("I have more money at home" when he doesn't) so she'll lend Harvey the money.

But Harvey does have choices. Each family might handle the situation differently. Talk about several options and how desirable and feasible you think each option is. For example, Harvey could:

- Wait and not get the tape today. He could ask his mom to bring him to the record store the following week after he gets his next allowance.
- Call his mom from the store and ask if he can borrow the money from his friend's mom.
- Ask to borrow the money from his friend's mom and explain that he can repay her next week after he gets his allowance.

Stretching It

Come holiday time, kids, like adults, are pressed for funds and find it hard to figure out how much to spend for each person on their list. To help, suggest they fill in this chart:

1. How much money I have saved for presents ____________
2. How much money I plan to save for presents ____________
3. Total of how much money I will spend for presents (Add 1 and 2) ____________
4. How much I can spend for each gift I'm giving ____________

I'm giving a gift to . . .	*How much I can afford to spend*
1. ____________	____________
2. ____________	____________
3. ____________	____________
4. ____________	____________
5. ____________	____________
Total: (Should not be more than the total in #3)	____________

It's Your Choice

When a character in a story you're reading to your child has a choice to make, stop reading and, in language the child understands, ask him to:

- Retell the situation the character finds herself in.
- Talk about the people, things and ideas that the character should think about before deciding what to do next.
- Think about what he would do in the situation.

Then, as you read on, talk about what the child chose to do as compared to what the character chose to do.

A list of books that are specifically designed to help children understand the consequences of choices is found in Appendix I, "Great Books for Children."

Spending Survival Guide

Encourage your children to use humor and creativity when looking at his own spending mistakes. Jessie, age eight, has had a "Spending Survival Guide" since second grade. Here's what a year's worth of mistakes have netted him:

1. Used the money mom gave me to by juce and milk at the store for chips and soda. When she found out, I got screemed at and had to go back to the store and by juce and milk with my own money. Better do what mom says when it s her money.

2. I had 2 weeks to buy Billy a Mets baseball hat for his birthday with the $6 mom gave me. (He loves the Mets!) When I got to the store that morning, they were all out of Mets caps. I had to buy him one with the Pitsburg Pirats on it. Better buy what I want when I see it next time.

Want It-Need It Game

Six- and seven-year-olds can play this game with each other. You can jot down the following list of items and ask each child to think about which is a need or a want (or neither) to him. If it's a need for neither, ask what type of person it might be a need for.

Use the children's answers to explore why they think something is a want or a need.

WANT IT-NEED IT GAME

Item	First Child	Second Child	A Need for Whom?
Space suit			
Swimming ability			
Friendship			
Doctor			
Training in sign language			
Winter jacket			
Sled			
Eye glasses			
Blood transfusion			
Bicycle			
Computer			
Ability to hunt			
Wheelchair			
Large-screen television			
Alarm clock			
Sneakers			
Stuffed animals			
(Add any of your own items.)			

Chapter Five

Earning Money

Making It the Old-Fashioned Way – With Some Twists

Scene: Ten-year-old Ginny is complaining to her mother.

Ginny: "I don't understand it. All the other kids are making extra money doing things for the neighbors. How come nobody ever asks me even to walk their dog or water their plants when they go on vacation?

Your Choice of Responses

You can say:

1. "Why would anyone ask you to do anything? You won't even walk our dog without a fuss."
2. "You don't have to work. If you need more money, ask and we'll give it to you."
3. "I don't understand what's bothering you—not having enough money or feeling slighted by not being asked to do something?"
4. "Let's sit down and discuss how you can change the situation."

A LOOK BEHIND THE RESPONSES

Choice (1) may be accurate, but it doesn't do anything to foster self-esteem; instead it heightens the child's doubts about herself. Choice (2) misleads the child. It assumes no intrinsic connection between work and money. Choice (3) is a good first step in exploring the problem. And choice (4) indicates you care enough about her concerns to help her discover her strengths and capitalize on them.

THE WORK-MONEY CONNECTION

Kids understand concrete connections. If you're a fire fighter and your children have seen you hose down blazes, they can visualize you at work. If you're a dentist and the children have visited your office or watched you examine a patient's mouth, they understand what you do (especially if you've tended to their teeth as well). But picture the five-year-old who goes to his father's office and hears his father argue with someone on the telephone or sees him sitting around a table talking to others about the price of paper. He has no idea that his father is the purchasing agent for a Fortune 500 company. How does the six-year-old who sees his mother at a desk, flipping through books and writing on a yellow pad, know that she's researching an important legal brief? When parents work in occupations where no product exists to be seen, touched or heard, they must *tell* their children what work they do. If it's impossible to bring your children to work with you occasionally, take them to your place of business on Saturday or Sunday, so they can picture where you are when you are not with them.

If kids don't understand exactly what parents do during the day, they are surely going to be vague about how this time away from home has anything to do with the candy they buy at the supermarket.

It's a parent's job to help children understand the work-money connection. Opportunities to discuss this arise all the time: When you take a child to work with you, when he wants something expensive and you've said no, or when you're in the midst of paying the monthly bills.

Let's run through one scenario. Abigail needs sneakers. Based on what you think you can afford, you tell her she can spend up to $45 for them. Abigail falls in love with the $95 pair and stews over the fact that you're not going to buy them for her. What a perfect time to explain what it takes to earn the additional $50, that it takes you from two to three hours of being away from the home to earn that and that the additional $50 is needed to pay for other, more essential things. If pressed to explain why you don't have enough money to buy everything the family wants, like her friend Sarah does, be honest. Your family doesn't earn as much money as Sarah's family.

Children don't base their love or respect on how much their mother or father earns. It's interesting to examine their perception of what different occupations *should* earn (as opposed to what they *do* earn). It is simpler and more personal than that of adults. We asked two six-member groups (one of eight-year-olds; one of eleven-year-olds) at the New Jersey YM-YWHA camps to tell us which of the following jobs they considered most important, and consequently, which should be paid the most.

Their answers were surprising. (Perhaps they are representative of their age groups across the country; perhaps not. This is a sample, not a scientific study.)

All the children in both groups considered these select occupations "most important" to our society: an elementary school teacher, a U.S. Senator, the President of the United States, a fire fighter, a police officer, a truck driver delivering food to supermarkets, a college professor, a day-care worker and a pediatrician. "Important," but not in the top rung, were parents who do housework, garbage collectors, plumbers and librarians. "Not so important," but not at the bottom of the list, were major league baseball players, presidents of large corporations, comic book writers and counterpeople at McDonalds. The only occupation listed that a majority of the children thought was "not at all important" was a model for a teen magazine.

Kids absorb their work attitudes and work ethics from people closest to them. Parents who enjoy work, take pride in the fact that they do something well, and share some of the problems and most of the triumphs tend to rear children who see working as exciting and rewarding. Even though parents may be unaware of the consequences, those who grumble about the boss, the company, the job and the pay are likely to raise children who are suspect about work. One small business consultant rhetorically asked a gathering of entrepreneurs if it was any wonder why entrepreneurs' kids shy away from the family business. "They hear their parents complain so often that they wonder what can be challenging, exciting or rewarding about something that causes so much consternation, annoyance and anguish."

In everyone's work experiences, there are times of frustration. Your children sense your irritation and exhaustion, even if you don't verbalize it. So it's important to explain what the problem is. Inevitably, they will want to know why you don't quit. Your answer might be that there are still satisfactions—salary, security or the prospect that this will lead to a more rewarding job.

THE FIRST EARNING EXPERIENCE: WORK AT HOME

We don't believe in paying children for routine chores that family members do simply because they are family members—making beds, picking up and putting away toys, hanging up their clothes, helping with dishes after dinner, walking the dog and so forth. We certainly do not want to rear a child who asks "How much are you going to pay me?" when we ask him to take out the garbage or help empty the dishwasher.

Does that mean we don't pay children for tasks done around the house?

No.

While we don't want children to expect to be paid for everything they do, when children are too young to work outside the home, paying for *extra* tasks—those your children aren't regularly responsible for, such as repotting plants or washing cars—is a good way for them to earn extra money. It helps them feel independent, raises their confidence in their abilities and becomes the genesis of understanding the money-to-labor ratio: that "fun dollars" come from hard work.

Tips on Making the Experience a Good One

If you do hire your children, think of the experience as a business transaction with a bit of value-training thrown in—simply because you're the parent.

1. Be as specific as you can when explaining what needs to be done. Instructing a child to "clean the garage" leads to a lot of misinterpretation. What parent has the same definition of "clean" as the child! Set the parameters: Do you want the tools rearranged, the floor swept, scraps of lumber thrown out? Where should the trash go? How long do you expect the task will take? When do you want it finished? After you've given the instructions, ask your child to review the process with you to make certain you both understand and agree how the job is to be performed. You may have to work with her for a while if she needs help in figuring out how to do something—especially if it's something she's never done before.

2. Give children considerable leeway in making the job interesting and creative for themselves. Your objective is to have the job completed in a way that satisfies you. If the children decide to play in the pile of leaves they've just raked before they bag them, then let them. Shouldn't there be an element of fun in work? If your son decides to take the screens out and wash them on the lawn with a hose instead of in the tub as you suggested, think of it as an imaginative way of handling the situation, rather than as a rebuttal to your instructions.

3. Evaluate your child's job performance. Performance at school is evaluated; job performance should be, too. Keep your expectations as high as your child's ability will allow. If your daughter knows the difference between weeds and flowers in the garden, but this time she leaves a patch of weeds because she's distracted by the music she's listening to, don't pay her until it's done. If your son doesn't wash the car as you wanted, show him what he missed and ask him to follow up on that. Similarly, if the job is done well, be lavish with your appreciation. Your encouragement is worth even more than the money paid.

4. Pay by the job—not by the hour. Children work at varying

speeds and with various levels of thoroughness. Some kids work slowly because they dawdle; others work slowly because they're meticulous. Some work quickly because they're efficient; others because they're slipshod. So an hourly rate just doesn't work with kids. (And be certain you're paying a realistic rate for the job. What would you have to pay a stranger to do the same job?)

5. Diversify, diversify, diversify. Kids like variety and challenge. Girls like to do jobs that are often offered to boys (like mowing the lawn) and boys like to try their hand at traditionally "girl" jobs (like cleaning closets). They also like demanding tasks for which they have to exercise new skills and hidden aptitudes. Your ten-year-old daughter might have a penchant and a talent for painting that neither of you realized before she took on the assignment of staining the porch stairs.

Encouragement or Praise?

As parents we wear two hats when we employ our children. First, as boss of the project, we're in charge and ultimately responsible for its completion. Second, as parents, we want to make the experience one that fosters the child's self-esteem, confidence and feelings of worth. To do both, we want to approach children in a way that says to them, "You are capable—go ahead and try." Psychologist Don Dinkmeyer sees a subtle, but important, difference between praise and encouragement.

Praise	*Encouragement*
"You did a great job in painting the underside of the steps."	"I can see it took great ingenuity to paint the underside of the steps. You must have really worked hard on that."

While both praise and encouragement focus on positive behavior, what are the fine differences between the two?

Praise	*Encouragement*
Focuses on what someone else thinks of the child.	Focuses on what the child thinks of himself.
Rewards only well-done tasks. Implies "If you haven't done it right, then there is nothing positive in what you've done.	Provides recognition for effort and improvement.

Discourages attempts to try when it looks like you might fail.	Helps to develop the courage to be imperfect and the willingness to try new ideas.

Encouragement requires careful listening to what you're saying and to what your child is saying, focusing on your child's assets—not necessarily on accomplishments—and recognizing efforts and contributions that went into the job. It also creates opportunities for a good laugh together. "I never saw anyone paint the underside of steps upside down. I think you've developed a whole new painting specialty."

Things to Consider

When two people make an agreement where one is to complete a task satisfactorily in exchange for money provided by the other, they're entering into a contract. When the worker is a child, important questions are raised.

Does a child have a right to refuse a paid job? Technically, yes. Just as you can refuse to work for someone for whatever reason, your child can turn down your offer. Perhaps he just doesn't want to be bothered. Or he'd rather be with his friends this Saturday morning. Or he'd rather do anything else than sort through supermarket coupons. Or, simply, he doesn't need the money.

If you really need the job done, don't make this a business offer. If the guest room needs a top-to-bottom cleaning because your aunt and uncle are unexpectedly stopping over tonight, the kids *have to* help you out. While you're at the airport, they must air the blankets, vacuum, clean up the mess and make the beds. No *ifs*, *ands* or *buts*. And also no pay. Pitching in during times of pressure is what family members are supposed to do for each other.

What if you can't afford to pay for out-of-the-ordinary tasks children need to help with? There are many ways to say "thank you" for doing something extra. Perhaps your son wants to go the basketball game on Saturday but doesn't have a way of getting there. Make certain you drive him. Other rewards could include more time with you, a note on his pillow telling him how much you appreciate all he does, a plate of his favorite brownies at dinner the next night.

What if the child has been offered another job but you need her to do something for you instead? What happens when both you and the neighbor need your daughter to babysit for a couple of hours in the afternoon? Your neighbor would pay her, but you weren't going to. Assuming that you can afford it, matching the payment she would normally receive from someone else seems fair.

BRANCHING OUT: WORKING OUTSIDE THE HOME

All of us remember the thrill we experienced the first time someone other than our parents paid us for something we made, sold or did. Today's kids aren't much different. They, too, can feel their self-esteem rise when they earn money, feeling monetarily independent (in their terms) from their parents.

No magic age exists for kids to begin looking outside the home for a job. A responsible eight-year-old can help out a vacationing neighbor by watering plants, bringing in the mail or caring for caged pets. Ten-year-olds can run errands for neighbors, collect cans and bottles, or even start their own little businesses.

Helping Kids Find Job Opportunities

For the most part, children don't really need to support themselves. Since the money they earn is usually "extra," they can be testers, trying on different jobs to see which one best fits their individual personalities and talents.

There are "Would you rather . . ." questions we can ask our children to help them identify their strengths and search for work in areas they will enjoy. You can make up your own or use the ones below to get the process started. As you run through them, have your children jot down their answers, so they can return to this sheet as a reference from time to time since their answers will change from year to year and you don't want them pigeonholed simply because at age seven they had a particular leaning. The leaning might be altogether different five years later.

Would you rather . . .

1. Act in a school play?
2. Teach the alphabet to a young child?
3. Carve an animal out of wood?

1. Figure out a hard math problem?
2. Make your own greeting cards?
3. Play an instrument in a band?

1. Write an article for the school paper?
2. Learn about weather stations?
3. Learn how banks make a profit?

1. Sell magazines to your neighbors?
2. Prepare a party for your friends?
3. Do experiments with batteries and bulbs?

1. Take telephone messages?
2. Read a story to a blind person?
3. Care for your mom's plants?

When you grow up, would you rather . . .

1. Defend a client in court?
2. Explore different countries?
3. Do research on cancer?

1. Dive for pearls?
2. Work as a TV cameraperson?
3. Sell new breakfast cereals to people?

1. Give haircuts?
2. Address envelopes?
3. Work in a department store?

1. Take passport photos?
2. Help alcoholics with their problems?
3. Work with others to develop a TV commercial?

These and other "Would you rather . . ." questions help children discover if they like selling, collecting, making things, cleaning things, inventing things, performing, interacting with people, organizing, etc.

They also identify how children like to operate. Do they prefer to work indoors or outdoors? Do they prefer working with older people, with their peers, or alone? Do they want to work for someone else? Would they prefer to set up their own business? Would they be willing to work on a commission basis or must they be assured of money for a task done?

Also consider the practical considerations.

1. Do they want or need a steady job (say babysitting every Tuesday and Thursday after school)? Can they be available for

work whenever someone calls (such as on an occasional Saturday evening)?

2. How much time do they have for work each week? Will work cut into or eliminate afterschool programs or free time?

3. What are they good at? Do they have particular skills or talents people will pay for? Ability to explain complex math formulas might translate into tutoring. Ability to get people to laugh might translate into dressing up as a clown and performing at little kids' birthday parties. Ability to mend things might translate into a neighborhood toy-fixing business.

Job Hunting Strategies

Jobs for preteens are difficult to get simply by asking or applying for them. People are inclined to hire children under age fourteen only if they feel the kids are responsible or have "proven" themselves. Yet children want to work and there are many things for which they are well-suited. Here are a few job-hunting strategies for this age group.

Show off

1. Do your own thing and do it well. If neighbors see a youngster mowing his parent's lawn, watering plants or weeding, they are more likely to ask him to take care of their lawn. If they see the child is good with cats, dogs or other animals, they will be more likely to hire him if they need a dog walker, cat sitter, birdcage cleaner or gerbil feeder when they go away.

2. Befriend the kids in the neighborhood. If your child would like a babysitting or mother's helper job, suggest she play with the neighbor's young children. If she can show the children's parents she is responsible and that the children like her and enjoy being with her, she will probably be tapped as the children's babysitter.

Use your senses

1. Keep an *eye* on the neighbors' property. Suggest that your child look around at the neighbors' homes for what needs to be done (raking, weeding, sweeping walks and driveways, shoveling snow, etc.). Many people hate doing these chores themselves and are willing to pay a reasonable rate to have them done for them.

2. Keep a keen *ear* out for what the neighbors are saying. If a child hears a neighbor mention that a job needs doing (watering

plants while the family is on vacation, for example), the child has a perfect opportunity to get the job.

Spread the word

1. Be a big mouth. Networking starts early in life. For example, Julie tells her parents' friends that she loves teaching young children how to use computers and how she'd like to start a tutoring business. Word spreads and before Julie knows it, she's gotten a passel of little pupils clamoring for lessons.

2. Be a kid welcome-wagoneer. New people in the neighborhood are usually overwhelmed by the move and are grateful for helping hands to unpack boxes, throw out garbage, sweep the attic or watch the kids for a few moments. If your child volunteers to help with these chores (without pay, of course), then the next time the neighbor needs help around the house, your child will probably get a call—this time as a paid assistant.

Be a trainee

1. Start as a sibling helper. Your child can assist an older brother or sister who is being paid for babysitting or gardening. Then the next time a neighbor calls and the older sibling is busy, the younger one will become the alternate choice.

2. Do it for free and for fun. Even when children in this age group cannot get after-school or summer jobs, they can invest in the future by acquiring skills and testing different occupations. They can apprentice as an assistant to a magician, volunteer at the library, or cook dinner for an elderly infirmed neighbor. These things are fun to do, are enriching and may provide a child with future recommendations.

Entrepreneurism: Starts With a Lemonade Stand and Gets Sweeter

Parents whose children show an entrepreneurial or a creative bent will want to encourage those tendencies.

- Children who love to write can collect news from neighbors and start a neighborhood newspaper that they sell.
- Kids who are good cooks can set up stands to sell their cookies and punch drinks; they can prepare and deliver dinners for working neighborhood parents or bake for charity sales.
- Children can fill needs that others won't. They can run kid-

walking services, taking little kids places when parents are too busy. They can clean attics and garages, collect recyclables or wash cars.

- Children who make fanciful craft creations—wonderful bracelets, earrings, painted T-shirts—can sell them.
- Children with a flair for photography can take pictures at community events and sell their photos to the subjects.
- Children good at writing limericks can team up with others who have good voices to create a singing telegram service.
- Children who are bilingual can tutor other children in a foreign language.
- Inventive children can invent. Just recently a twelve-year-old won an award for inventing a toilet seat that glowed in the dark (for all those children and adults who get up and go to the bathroom at night).

WORKING FOR THE COMMUNITY

Volunteer work is probably the best training ground for future employment and is an excellent opportunity to develop the foundation for a solid set of values. In general, children are moved by the plight of those in trouble, are aware of the environmental concerns surrounding the land, water, air and animals, and are eager to become part of the solutions to some of the world's ills.

Your children's involvement may take many forms: from fund-raising (everything from selling junk to "walking" for dollars) to hands-on participation (playing checkers with the elderly in a nursing home or helping to clear an unsightly abandoned lot).

Encouraging children to get involved is probably a parent's greatest contribution to the survival of the planet and of the human race.

THINGS TO WATCH FOR AS CHILDREN ENTER THE WORLD OF WORK

Working for money while growing up can be enriching, rewarding, character-building and fun. It can also be dangerous—and that's where parents have to step in.

Don't let work steal childhood from your youngster. Kids need time to play, daydream, and be with their friends and by themselves. During their school years, their first "responsibility" is as a student, not as a wage earner. It's important for parents to keep this in mind and make certain the balance of school, free time and earning time is in sync.

All jobs are not alike. Listen carefully when your child complains of something or someone in a work environment. Often, children complain because they're unfamiliar with the demands of the work world or because they are asked to do something they don't like to do. If your son complains that the neighbor isn't paying him for mowing the lawn even though he promised to come back tomorrow to finish the job, he might not realize that one gets paid only after a task is completed. If your daughter balks at having to play outside with the children she's caring for instead of watching cartoons on television with them, she might not realize that as the "employer," the children's mother has the right to make decisions about the welfare and the activities of the children.

Other times, youngsters just need someplace safe to vent frustrations—the type that we all feel when working. What better place than with a parent! This situation offers you an opportunity to help a child take someone else's view and to explore creative alternatives: "Why do you think the neighbor wants his money back because the bracelet you made for her daughter broke? How would you feel if that happened to you? What else can you do for her? How important is it that she be satisfied with your work?"

Still, there are times when a child's complaint signals danger—the type that the child might not even be aware of but which you, as an adult, sense.

Perhaps she's complaining that the mother she's helping for the summer wants her to watch the three-year-old by the pool, but the toddler runs around and always plays close to the edge of the deep end. "I'm petrified. I don't know how to swim well. What if he falls in," she worries aloud, afraid to tell her employer that the responsibility is too much for her. If she's not comfortable talking to her employer about that, you should step in.

Perhaps your daughter complains that the store owner, for whom she stocks shelves, is always leaning over her and seems to brush up against her at every opportunity. She's uncomfortable about this and tells you about it. You must take her out of harm's way. As the guardian adult, you are responsible to tell the owner why you will not let your daughter work there anymore.

Perhaps the people who pay your son to babysit for their child tell him they'll be home at 10 P.M., but they consistently come home between 11:30 and midnight—even though your son has told them he has to be home at 10 P.M. on weeknights. You can't allow him to babysit for these people anymore because they are taking advantage of him.

Use these early, negative job experiences to teach some basic employment principles and practices: As an employee, you needn't be subjected to poor treatment, sexual harassment or forced to do things that are dangerous, immoral or illegal.

Help your child negotiate fair payment for his work. When a child protests that he's not getting paid enough for what he's doing, he may be right. (Many employers try to take advantage of kids who are unsure of their talents and their rights, unsophisticated about wages, and uncomfortable about asking for more money.) Your child says he wants to quit. Explain that if he likes the job, he has a number of options besides quitting. If he's helping parents at toddler birthday parties, for example, he can offer to do the decoration or the clean-up as well (thus increasing the number of hours he's working). He can negotiate an increase based on the number of children at the party: His rate for five or fewer children is $5 per hour; if the number of children at the party exceeds five, the hourly rate increases $.50 per child. After doing some research about what other kids his age are charging, he can simply raise his hourly rate, citing his research. He could raise his rate after a year and simply tell his prospective customers that he is experienced in this area and is now charging an additional one dollar an hour.

We said earlier that earning money does much to enhance children's self-esteem—not to mention their feeling of financial independence. But it does more. It helps children understand the connection between work and money. It helps them understand what we as parents do every day. It puts children in touch with others with different perspectives and backgrounds. Lastly, it teaches them to shoulder responsibility, to stand up for themselves and to establish good work habits—values that will serve them well as they grow into adulthood.

ACTIVITIES

Sweet and Smart Entrepreneuring

Suppose your child wants to set up the typical "first business"—a cold drink stand. Rather than planting her outside your house, supplying her with the lemonade, cups and napkins, and allowing her to keep the money collected, turn the experience into a learning situation.

• **Location.** Ask her to write down places where people might get thirsty or might want to stop for a drink: At the playground where people take small children? At the park where the high school kids play basketball? In front of your house? In front of a luncheonette? Near the entrance to the library?

When you ask children to think about how they can maximize sales, they'll realize quickly that the location of the business is of prime importance.

• **Product.** What kind of drinks should she sell? There are two things to consider: what people want to drink and the cost of providing the drink.

The child could buy cans of soda from the supermarket. If she buys by the case, she might find that each can costs $.23 and that she can probably sell each for $.40. Then, she can figure what her profit would be on each can.

Or she could make her own drinks and buy the cups and the ice she'll need. Because she has an older brother and sister, she knows teens like lemonade and grape drink. If she decides to locate where the teens are most likely to buy, that's what she should consider selling. But if she decides to locate where adults will be buying the drinks for young children, ask her what factors would go into their buying decisions. (They probably won't want grape drink because it's too messy and little ones might prefer sweeter drinks like juice rather than something tart like lemonade. Perhaps orange and pineapple juices diluted would be best.)

If she makes her own drinks, she has to figure out how much each will cost to make (ingredients, cups and ice) and what she can sell a cup for. Then she can figure how much profit she will make from each cup (price minus cost equals profit).

What she has to decide is which of the products, canned soda or homemade drinks, will sell best and which product will net the most profit?

• **Market Research.** Will enough people buy the drinks? Ask her to think of ways to find out. (She could test her stand at different times of the day, in different locations, using different drinks.) If one of the drinks turns out to be a terrific seller and one of the areas is full of customers at a certain time of day, then she knows she has a profitable, thrist-quenching business that meets the needs of its customers.

Pet Service Businesses

Suppose your child wants to capitalize on his love of animals and wants to start a business caring for other people's pets. Here's a business plan you could help him follow as he explores the possibility.

- **Market Survey.** How can he find out if people want to use his service? (She could knock on neighbors' doors and ask them, develop a questionnaire and put it in neighbors' mailboxes, or phone and ask them.)
- **Setting a Price.** He has to figure out how complicated each job is and how much time each would take to do. Then he has to determine a fair hourly rate for his service—not too much under or too much over what other people in the neighborhood charge for similar services. Walking dogs for half an hour when he gets home from school may be worth $2 a walk; cleaning out birdcages every week might be worth $5 each time.
- **Advertising.** He must get the word out or no one will know what he's doing. Should he call people? Make up flyers and distribute them? Put an announcement on a local bulletin board? Make an announcement at a community meeting? Give a stack of flyers to the local veterinarian?

Does he have a catchy name for his business? Does he describe his business well? Do potential customers have his name and phone number? Will they keep it in a handy place? How can his advertising help them remember his services?

- **Keeping the books.** Even before your son has his business up and running, show him how to keep track of what he earns. Since he has no product costs (his time, expertise and reliablity are what people pay for), his weekly accounting is very simple. Use a chart with the following column heads: *Job*, *Time Spent* and *Income*.

This will help him to adjust his prices to accurately reflect how much time he spends on each job. He'll learn quickly that all birdcage cleaning is not alike. If he's taking two hours to clean out a birdcage that houses ten birds, he can't charge the same as for a cage housing one bird that takes fifteen minutes. He'll have to adjust his price accordingly.

Chapter Six

Saving and Investing

Helping Kids Think Beyond Today

Scene: Alex hands his mother a $25 check.
Seven-year-old Alex: "Mom, may I please have real money for this check grandpa John and grandma Alice gave me for my birthday?"

Your Choice of Responses

You can:

1. Say "yes" and hand $25 to him, telling him to enjoy spending it.
2. Say "no" and march the check to the bank where you'll put it in a savings account for his college education.
3. Cash the check for him but use this as the springboard for a discussion about saving.

A LOOK BEHIND THE RESPONSES

Choice (3) has the right elements. Small amounts of money given as a gift to a child are technically the child's to spend or save. But as a parent you have a responsibility to offer guidance and advice because you understand the value of saving.

WHAT IS SAVING?

"Be real," you might say. "Everyone knows what saving is—the act of putting money away." But for what? Is money to be put away for all time? Absolutely not. Even those adults who drop money into saving accounts "for a rainy day" know that sooner or later "it pours" and the money is spent or allocated for a particular purpose. Saving is really "spending deferred."

Children enjoy the idea of saving if they realize that the money being put away is for something to be bought or used later, for something they really want or need. When a family talks openly about how they're saving for a new car, for example, and how, because of it, they'll be making some financial sacrifices, children might not immediately understand the connection. When they see the bright, shiny red car in the driveway many months later, they see the family's excitement over it and sense the connection between the car and the family's not going to McDonald's as much in recent months.

It's Not Just About Money

Putting money away for some later expenditure is a powerful experience on many levels. A child with control over her own savings feels in control of at least one aspect of her life. Without that feeling, she may lose interest in the whole process of saving because she doesn't have a say in how much is saved and for what future purpose.

And if she doesn't understand the real meaning of what she's doing, she may become a miser, stashing money away for no purpose. Then, as she watches other kids spend their saved dollars on things they savor, she may feel a sense of deprivation because she doesn't dare spend the money.

Putting off satisfaction (not denying it) makes sense on other levels. It teaches children that:

1. People can't always have what they want when they want it. Just as you can't buy every piece of furniture you'd like to have in your home now, Joanne has to learn to put on hold her desire to buy those beautiful shells for her collection until she can afford to pay for them.

2. People have to decide what is most important to purchase now and what can wait. Anytime you can't have everything you want when you want it, you must set priorities. Learning how to do that will help a child in every aspect of life.

3. Planning is necessary. Knowing what you want first is important; so is charting a way to achieve it. If Billy wants to have enough money to buy his parents and siblings Christmas gifts, he has to think ahead. Will he need to save $2, $3 or $4 a week for the next three months? How will he do this? Through allowance? With money gifts saved from his birthday? With money he's earned?

4. Saving allows for a change of heart. Many of us remember a time (perhaps not that long ago) when the $20 in our pocket was just itching to be spent. And we obliged. Quickly. Then, a short time later, we regretted the expenditure because we found something to do or buy that was more important to us.

5. There's a special joy that comes from getting something you've waited for. Who can't recall (with a rush of emotion) one special childhood item we waited and waited for and the thrill that came from finally getting it. For one youngster, the supreme moment came when she put a beautiful $22 stamp from France into her stamp album, a stamp that the dealer held for her for six weeks—the time she needed to save for it. For her sister, it was squirreling away enough money so that she could buy the three stuffed pigs she had fallen in love with three months earlier and perch them on a shelf above her bed.

For Kids, What's "Later" Mean?

We've talked before about how children under the age of five really don't have a clear concept of "later." Tomorrow might be understood by older toddlers as the time after they go to sleep, but saving money for 7 tomorrows, 14 tomorrows or 365 tomorrows is too abstract to comprehend.

By the time children are six, they have a better understanding of time. They listen to stories about their past and can penetrate the mysteries of the future by the sequence of significant holidays (dad's birthday is in two weeks, Halloween is in twelve days). They are also eager for possessions (though, of course, they're not very respectful of them) and can be great little savers (though indecisive spenders).

Eight-year-olds are becoming more grown-up in their relation to the outside world. They have learned to wait. They like the idea of being rewarded, especially with money, and many like to watch their savings grow to a certain point before they spend it—frequently on treating friends or buying an item to add to their collection.

Introduction-to-Saving Tips

Given these general characterizations based on age, how do we as parents introduce the concept of saving?

From one day to the next, and then stretch it a little longer. When a child is working on Thanksgiving crafts projects at school and circling the calendar to "see" how many days until "turkey Thursday," he is aware of short intervals between today and another day. That's when it's appropriate to begin the saving process; perhaps by suggesting that if he puts away part of this week's allowance until next week, he can buy the packet of baseball cards he wants. Then, as his taste in acquisitions becomes more expensive (and you can bet it will), you can introduce a longer saving period. "If you put aside $2.50 a week, let's see how many weeks it'll be before you can buy the $12 crystal ring."

From the visual and concrete to the abstract. Let's give a rousing, elbow-bending "yes" to manufacturers who are bringing back glass piggy banks with easily removable rubber plugs. (One has to wonder what manufacturers had in mind when they developed banks you had to destroy in order to get at the money. Was it another indication of planned obsolescence or was it the manifestation of the mistaken idea that saved money is never to be spent?) And another enthusiastic "yes" to the parents who create their own piggy banks out of glass jars because they know that kids need to watch their savings grow and like to take the money out to count it.

HOW MUCH TO SAVE?

Just as there is no uniform percentage of saving for adults, none exists for children. Kids who are given more allowance than they need each week should be able to save. Those who have every dime accounted for cannot reasonably be expected to keep meaningful sums in reserve. The older the child and the more able she is to work for extra money, the more savings she can accrue.

When there is "extra money," such as earnings from lawn-mowing or dog-walking, kids should be encouraged to save at least part of the money instead of spending it all on tapes, food and movies. Because kids old enough to earn money are beginning to understand the value of having extra cash handy, most take to saving. Those who are tempted to spend as fast as they earn are often left disillusioned. Just when they need or want the extra money, they find themselves broke. One kid phrased it this way after he had frittered away all his summer earnings on snacks and little things he could no longer remember: "Next year more money will go into the piggybank's mouth than into mine."

One Family's "Three-Jar-Savings"

Some families have definite rules for saving, though children have complete autonomy over the saving goal (barring anything the parents think is immoral or the law says is illegal, of course). One family has its Three-Mason-Jar method, which is usually started when a child turns eight and begins earning extra money around the house.

In bright colors, the child labels three mason jars: "Fun Money," "Things and Places Money" and "Big Goals."

Fun Money is for spending on anything the child wants right away. Movies, money for the mall, baseball cards and sodas are all "fun money" items.

Things and Places is for short-term goals. Pictures of those things the child wants to save for—a skateboard, a new baseball glove, a new sweater, a compact disc, flowers for grandma for her sixty-fifth birthday—are cut out and pasted on the jar to visually remind the child of the goal.

Big Goals is for long-term saving. This jar, too, has to have a spending goal attached to it that is written or pictured on the jar. Though most kids under twelve don't understand the concept of saving for college (it's too far away and too abstract), those with older siblings or cousins probably do, so for them saving for college may be a reality. If it isn't, other big items that kids save for include mountain bikes, skis and stereos.

In the Three-Mason-Jar method, all the money the child earns is divided this way: 30 percent in each jar and 10 percent to a charitable cause or to help a person in need (the charitable cause is one chosen by the child). The child is allowed to raid a shorter-term goal jar to meet the needs of a bigger goal (for example, he can take money away from the Fun Money jar for the Things and Places account so he can get a compact disc sooner), but isn't allowed to do the reverse (grab some money from the Things & Places jar for a candy bar).

Why is the Three-Mason-Jar method so successful? It's fun. It's visual. And it helps kids establish priorities. Beyond that though, kids thrill with a sense of accomplishment and achievement as they watch their jars fill and see their goals become reality.

DEVELOPING LIFELONG SAVING HABITS

Habits, good and bad, form early and are hard to break. One of the best habits we as parents can help our children develop is one of regular saving. Make it fun and make it routine if you want to make it happen.

Decide together how much should be saved. The percentage of how much she saves from gifts, jobs or her allowance will vary from job to job, gift to gift, and year to year, but it's important to establish it in advance of getting the money.

Take it off the top. Kids, like adults, postpone saving and find themselves without anything to save at the end of a time period. So help your child tuck money into savings first—before she does anything else.

Set target dates for a specific goal. If a child is saving for a video game accessory, suggest she find a picture of it and mark it with the date on which she hopes to purchase it. Have her keep her eye on the goal by tacking the picture up on the refrigerator door with a magnet or pinning it up on her bedroom door.

Encourage your child to start saving early for high-spending times like Christmas and Hannukah (or that month of the year when everybody seems to have a birthday or an anniversary).

Encourage a coin roundup. Kids who feel they're too old for piggy banks can drop their loose change into a jar or dish instead of leaving it in their jeans pockets to be lost in the washing process. Once every few weeks persuade them to roll up the coins in heavy paper coin rolls available from the bank. They'll be amazed at how much money can be made from collecting change—when it's done in a systematic way.

If your child shows signs of becoming a collector, encourage him to take good care of all he amasses, for it well might be an investment. Many avid young collectors of baseball cards, olympic paraphernalia, stuffed animals, comic books, rocks and more have realized a profit years later from their collections. Talk to your child about what constitutes value in a collection: condition of the collectibles and rarity. It's important to remember that saving really can be equated to amassing something of value, whether it's money *or* something else.

Share some "trick-yourself-into-saving" techniques that you've picked up over the years: putting a portion of an allowance (in your case a paycheck) away each week; saving *all* your earnings from holiday gifts; spending less on yourself; tackling extra household chores; getting money into savings quickly before you have time to spend it; sharing movie popcorn with a friend rather than getting a whole carton for yourself; keeping a minimum amount of money in your pocket (the "what-you-don't-have-you-won't-spend" subterfuge).

Encourage your child to make his own decisions when it comes to saving—even if that's not how you would do it or what you would save for. The merchandise she finally buys or the activity she uses the money for is not as important as the fact that she's taking charge of her own life and engaging in the saving *process.*

FROM PIGGYBANK TO SAVINGS BANK . . . AND BEYOND

Sometime between the ages of six and ten, when children master the idea of saving for some future outlay, when they're old enough to sign their name legibly, and when they have saved a substantial sum (or you are ready to make a contribution to help them reach the hefty minimum opening deposit of most banks), they're ready for their first banking experience—opening an account in their own name.

Adult spadework for this important event starts with trying to find a child-friendly bank, not a small feat at a time when many institutions no longer accept what they consider piddling opening deposits (anything under $250) or they charge outrageous fees because they say small accounts are costly to service. Seek out an institution convenient to your home, so the child can eventually go by himself to make deposits or withdrawals. Credit unions are often more accommodating than banks, so if you belong to one, check its savings account policy.

Before you actually make the trip to a bank, it makes sense to explain some basic banking principles. If your child has follow-up questions or is still hazy about what's happening, the bank officer should take the time to explain the process.

Banking basic to review with kids:

A bank is a safe place for people to keep their money. Despite the banking failures we've had in recent years, that's still true if the institution is federally insured—commercial banks by the Federal Deposit Insurance Corporation (FDIC), savings banks by the Federal Savings and Loan Insurance Corporation (FSLIC) and credit unions by the National Credit Union Share Insurance Fund.

Banks add to depositor's money by giving them interest, something piggy banks don't do. "What's interest?" the kids are sure to ask. Your explanation: Banks do not put all their depositors' money into the vault. Instead they pool the money and lend some of it for a year or more to people who want to borrow money to buy homes or cars or to start businesses. And they charge these people a rental fee for borrowing money, the same way you're charged a fee when you rent a home video. The fee that banks charge people who borrow the money is called interest. The fee that banks pay you for allowing them to lend your money to others is also called interest. To make its profit, the bank charges borrowers more interest than it pays to its depositors.

The money you deposit is yours to withdraw at any time.

Beyond the Savings Account

If your child already has $250 in the bank and is interested in learning more about the other ways that money can grow when it's invested, you should discuss some investment possibilities.

U.S. Savings Bonds. They're safe, backed by the federal government, and can be bought at a bank for as little as $25. You can cash it in anytime after the first six months, but if you hold them for five years or more, they pay a minimum of 4 percent annually (as of March 1992). The rates on Savings Bonds are reset every six months, so find out the current rate of interest being paid by calling 800-US-BONDS (800-872-6637).

Money Market Accounts. Bank money market accounts require a large opening balance of $1,000 or more. Money market funds are also available through mutual fund companies and sometimes accept lower initial deposits than banks. The money market funds aren't insured the way most banks are, but they have been safe. Both money market accounts and funds pay a slightly higher rate of interest than savings accounts.

Certificates of Deposit (CDs). Talk to a kid about a CD and he'll think music, so you'll have to identify these CDs as certificates of deposit until he knows what you're talking about. Certificates of deposit allow the purchaser to lock in a given interest rate for a specific period of time. That works wonderfully if the interest rates are high when you make your initial investment and if they drop within the holding period. It doesn't work well if interest rates are low when you invest and climb during the holding period. Remember: Explain to your child that if he wants or needs his money before a CD comes due (six months, one year or five years from when he bought it), he'll have to pay a penalty. So CDs are definitely for money that's not needed right away.

Mutual Funds. There are hundreds of mutual fund companies with different funds that invest their money in a variety of ways: bonds, stocks, a combination of stocks and bonds, government securities, real estate, precious metals, international companies and more. A mutual fund pools and invests the money from all the people who invest in it. This is safer for a novice investor than buying individual stocks because the fund spreads the money among many investments, so there's less of a chance for a total wipeout.

Because there is no guarantee or insurance connected to mutual funds, youngsters have to understand that their money is at risk, that they can lose some or all of it as well as earn substantial profits if the value of the shares they own goes up.

ABOUT SAVING FOR COLLEGE

"College." The word itself strikes terror in the hearts of many parents because it looms as a major financial responsibility. Many parents stash away whatever money they can for it: lump sums—like tax refunds, cash gifts from relatives, even poker winnings—or regular fixed sums from paychecks. As the annual price of a higher education gets steeper, most of us feel frustrated, realizing we're not going to be able to save enough to provide all our kids with a loan-free, private college education when they're ready for it. We know children will have to help out with their own savings as well. Our anxiety is understandable, but our eagerness to get the children involved in working and saving for education should be kept in check until the child is old enough to understand what college is—usually when the child is in junior high school. Then the idea of higher education becomes especially alluring when they hear stories from older kids coming home from college—a sibling, a cousin or a neighbor.

Tips on Saving for College

Communicate openly about the family's financial position vis-à-vis college financing. As soon as possible, generally when the child is in junior high, discuss any financial limits on college costs and what will be expected from your child.

Work out a "matching grant" program. Watch your youngster's savings grow if you suggest that you'll match every dollar he saves for college.

Encourage excellence in whatever the child seems to have talent in. If your child has the potential for an academic or sports scholarship, encourage these activities. Scholarships are never sure bets. But they are even more remote if your child doesn't have the credentials for them.

Perhaps the greatest incentive children have to save for college is to see that you are doing the same. Because you've taught them that people save money for things that are important, your saving for their future sends a powerful message: Education is important and it's worth saving for.

ACTIVITIES

What a Difference a Bank Makes

Share with your child the chart at the bottom of this page of how money in a bank earns more money without him having to do anything. It tells you what $100 saved every year will add up to as the years go on, based on 5 percent interest compounded annually.

Year	Money saved per year	Amount Accumulated in a Bank at 5% Interest	Amount Accumulated at Home (No Interest)
1	$100.00	$105.00	$100.00
2	$100.00	$215.25	$200.00
3	$100.00	$331.11	$300.00
4	$100.00	$452.67	$400.00
5	$100.00	$580.30	$500.00
6	$100.00	$714.32	$600.00
7	$100.00	$855.04	$700.00
8	$100.00	$1,022.79	$800.00
9	$100.00	$1,157.93	$900.00
10	$100.00	$1,320.83	$1,000.00

The Banking Adventure

To a parent, going to the bank may seem like a nuisance; but, to a child, it's an adventure. Some preliminary work can be done by a parent to eliminate frustration and prepare the child for her first big role as an educated consumer:

- Call a couple of banks in the area ahead of time to find out if they're federally insured, if they encourage children's accounts, and what documentation you would have to have with you *if* your child was going to open an account with the bank.
- Use the following list of questions for your child to ask the bank officer and a chart to use to rank the different banks.

	First Bank	Second Bank	Third Bank
1. What is the minimum I need to open an account?	______	______	______
2. What is the interest the bank pays? (The higher the better.)	______	______	______
3. Do I start getting interest as soon as the money is deposited? ("Yes" is better than "no.")	______	______	______
4. How do I take money out of the bank?	______	______	______
5. How do I put money into the bank?	______	______	______
6. When is the bank open?	______	______	______
7. Can I send in checks for deposit by mail?	______	______	______
My assessment of the service and friendliness of the bank officer I spoke to. (Very good, good, fair, poor.)	______	______	______

MY DECISION
I'm going to open up a savings account at ______________________________
because ______________________________

Chapter Seven

Consumerism

Helping Kids Become Smart Shoppers

Scene: Eight-year-old John is talking to his father.

John: You see this box of candy I bought at the movie theater? They charged $1.50 for this box, which I couldn't finish anyway. It's a rip. I can get the same candy in the supermarket for sixty cents.

Your Choice of Responses

You can:

1. Insist John bring candy or popcorn from home each time he goes to the movies.
2. Tell him he's wrong. The box of candy you get at the supermarket is smaller.
3. Take the supermarket candy out of the pantry and suggest that he look more carefully at both packages.
4. Remind him that you had told him not to buy candy at the movies.

A LOOK BEHIND THE RESPONSES

Insisting that John change his buying habits (1) or telling him he made a mistake to buy the candy at the theater (2) and (4) don't have the impact that firsthand discovery has. Instead, encourage him to check the pantry to compare the amount, price and quality of the theater candy with supermarket candy (3). That will have a lasting learning effect.

KIDS AS CONSUMERS

Kids are big spenders. They get their money from allowances, gifts from relatives, and workfare (payment for performing chores). Annually, they spend a total of $1.15 billion on apparel, $2.6 billion on play items such as toys and bikes, $3.2 billion on food and beverages, $797 million on movies and spectator sports, and $620 million at the video arcade—to name but a few of the major categories, according to James McNeal, marketing professor at Texas A&M University, who studies the spending habits of children.

All this spending doesn't take into consideration the influence kids have on their parent's consuming habits, such as which cereal or backpacks to buy, how the family will spend its vacation, or what brand of computer will go into the family room.

With that kind of spending clout, it's best that kids become savvy consumers around the time they purchase their first yo-yo.

TV: The Commercial Monster

Peeling kids away from the TV was a parental chore in the 1950s when we were the tykes and the set was on only four hours and thirty-five minutes per day. The job seems even more formidable today since the television is on an average of seven and a half hours per day. Statisticians tell us that between ages one and seventeen, the average youngster has seen 350,000 commercials (four hundred per week!). Not all the commercials are directed to them, either. When they come in to talk to parents who are watching TV, subtle commercial messages filter through. Beautiful women advertising cars implies that you, too, will be beautiful if you buy this auto.

Even government's watchdog, the Federal Trade Commission (FTC), which is supposed to keep an eye on the truth of the ads that appear on television, doesn't always catch misleading advertising. Sometimes parts of a toy seem to move by themselves; sometimes the words *batteries not included* flash across the screen too quickly or are too tiny for young readers to pick up easily; sometimes the commercial itself is so slick that it glosses over the caveats.

If the FTC can miss these subtle deceptive messages, kids certainly can. Television, radio and print ads are the backdrop for their viewing, listening and reading pursuits. Subtly and not-so-subtly, "buy" messages penetrate. Gloss, excitement, color and pizzazz make children vulnerable to buying first, examining later. So they make scads of buying mistakes: They find the big box of candy, once opened, is only half filled. The fan club that seems to send all sorts of wonderful stuff for its $17 initiation fee provides them with a shirt, photo and piles of advertising literature. The jeans that look great on the model pull in the crotch. The truck that seemed to be motorized in the ad needs a battery pack—at an additional $38—to get it going into high gear. After a few of these disappointing buying encounters, kids are primed to become smart consumers.

The "QUEF" Factor

We can help our children gain an understanding of *value* (which is what makes a good consumer) by helping them understand that it's not just Fun they're buying. It's the whole QUEF—Quality, Usefulness, Expense *and* Fun.

Quality depends on what you're examining, of course.

For clothes, kids should be told to examine how strong the fabric is, if the seams are tight, if there are many loose threads, if the zipper moves smoothly, if the washing instructions are clear.

For food items, kids need to know to use some of their senses:

smell, taste and sight. If food smells, tastes or looks "funny," it probably shouldn't be eaten. They should check ingredients, understanding that the first ingredient listed is the ingredient of greatest proportion in the food.

For entertainment expenditures, they have to decide if one amusement park has longer, better rides than another, if the reviews of one movie sound better to them than the reviews of another, if the seats for the ball game are good and the teams playing can be expected to produce an exciting event.

For play items, kids need to look at how toys are built and if they'll fall apart after a few weeks; if the game is interesting, has pieces that are sturdy, and can be conveniently stored; if the toys have all the pieces they should have to operate and will perform dependably time after time.

Usefulness doesn't apply to all items on which we spend our money. There are certain things we buy because we need them and will use them. (Usefulness is the major force when we say we "need" something.) Other things we buy because we want to look at them (collector dolls, posters), want to touch them (polished worry stones), want to taste them (ice cream) or want them to make us feel good (a puppy). But if we're buying something because we think it will be useful, just how useful will it be?

Expense is an important element in the mix because no matter how fine something is made, how much we can use it, and how dependable it is, if we can't afford it, we have to seek other options. And children have to understand this. Perhaps they'll have to sacrifice quality or dependability. Perhaps they should compare prices to see if the item can be bought for less elsewhere or perhaps they'd best not buy it at the moment.

Fun, like usefulness, is not a factor in every purchase, but when it is, let the good times roll and roll and roll. It's certainly a major component in "wanting" something. Something that's fun to eat, do, wear or have should be dependable fun for as long as we chomp on it, engage in it, wear it or own it. Fad-buying, the impulse-buying kids are so susceptible to, has that momentary high of making them feel they belong. But fads fizzle quickly, so kids who buy into all of them are left without funds but with closets full of items that may have been used or worn once or twice. Not fun! Ask children to ask themselves if they really like and will use the trendy item. Urge them to wait a few weeks before they buy it.

It may well be that at the end of that time, they'll buy it. If they don't, they may find that the fun they're seeking is in having money to buy something more substantial.

Tips for Helping Kids Become Better Consumers

Before kids make the major purchase for which they have been saving their money, it makes sense to prime them on what goes into a smart purchase.

Talk about how to get the best item for the best price. Have they been to a number of stores and compared prices? Have they checked *Zillions—Consumer Reports for Kids* (back issues of these independent magazines are available in most libraries) to see if the item has been tested and rated as to its performance, price, dependability and durability? Have they asked people who have bought this item whether they would recommend it and, if not, why not?

Talk about specific questions they should ask themselves about the purchase. What features do different models have and do you need the model with the greatest number of features? Is the item well made? Easy to operate? Easy to repair?

Talk about the store's return policy. Because they are not experienced consumers, kids often buy things that aren't "right." Sometimes the thing itself is shoddy, defective or dangerous. Sometimes the child finds that once she gets it home, she doesn't like it, doesn't look good in it or can't use it—even though the quality is fine. So urge neophyte consumers to ask about the store's return policy immediately. Can they return something for store credit or money? Who's responsible for the item, the store or the manufacturer? If the manufacturer is responsible, is the product under a warranty (the company's guarantee that if an item or a part of it does not work or last as it should for a certain period of time, the item will be replaced or repaired)?

Remind them to *always* keep the sales receipt. Returning an item is always scary for someone who doesn't know the process. So verbally walk a child through it, suggesting that he start the process by taking the sales slip and the item first to the department where the item was purchased or to the store's customer service desk. It may be that the process will end there with store credit or money returned. If the item purchased is under warranty, find out if the store will return it to the manufacturer for you or if you have to do it yourself. You may want to accompany a child on his first return trip so the process doesn't seem so intimidating.

TRADING: A CHILD'S COMPLEX RECREATION

Trading is far more complicated than going to a store and paying the shopkeeper a set price for a standard item (which the child may have seen in other stores for the same or a slightly different price). Trading requires an understanding of value and a fairly well-developed sense of negotiating principles. Yet it's an activity children engage in often and enthusiastically. Kids swap a peanut butter and jelly sandwich for two cupcakes, two comic books for a fabric painting set, a T-shirt for a team cap, hoop earrings for a cat pin, a music box for a fanny pack, doing a sibling's chores for a week for the right to use her skis on the weekend.

The thrill of getting something the child wants by giving up something she doesn't want outweighs her fear of not getting a fair deal for herself.

Consider the "gold watch for two baseball cards" swap story that occurred when a young man was nine. It was the golden era of the Oakland Athletics and the boy yearned for Reggie Jackson and Rollie Fingers baseball cards. A ten-year-old in his school was willing to trade the two he had, but only for a watch. "No problem," the nine-year-old thought. "My father never wears the watch in the bottom drawer of the old chest. I'll trade that." When the swap was made, he showed his father his prizes and told him how he had gotten them. The watch was an heirloom worth many thousands of dollars and, needless to say, it took parental intervention to negate the deal and recover the bounty that had been so enthusiastically traded away.

Kids know the value of some items—marbles, toys, video games, music CDs—but they're unsophisticated about a wide variety of items outside their realm and they're unaware of the factors that go into the value of used items: the original price of items, their condition, the supply and demand factor. Knowing these characteristics will help them become better traders and will ensure that they get a fair deal for themselves, something they worry about as they become older.

As parents, we can help them understand these principles by taking our children on jaunts to flea markets, garage sales, auctions or antique shops. They can see us examine the merchandise, ask questions, offer a price, negotiate with the other party, and finally decide whether to buy the item.

The negotiating process is key to becoming a good consumer. Hearing a parent say to a flea market vendor that, while he likes the tobacco tin, he's not so fond of it that he's willing to pay the existing price suggests some valuable principles:

- A person who wants something badly is willing to pay more than a person who casually wants something.
- Nobody has to make the deal. A person can walk away if he feels he's being bullied, treated unfairly or can't afford the purchase.

When the parent suggests to a seller that by hauling the sofa away immediately the dealer will save $40 in crating fees, which could be applied to reducing the price, the child learns principles of negotiation:

- Options can be created that can make everyone feel like a winner.
- People are willing to negotiate on other things besides price, such as time saved, convenience and service.

SCAMS AND NEAR-SCAMS KIDS SUCCUMB TO

Until kids become adults, they are not subject to major scams mainly because they don't have access to large sums of money. But they're easy prey for street hucksters, phony charity promoters and misleading advertisers. We discovered many when we spoke to a number of fifth-grade classes:

The whipper that didn't. One girl who enjoyed cooking sent away for a beater advertised on television that would whip cold skim milk into a whipped cream consistency. Not so. The skim milk stayed skim.

The better-looking picture. Many children were disappointed by the items they sent away for mainly from cereal companies. The picture on the box looked better or more complex than what was received.

Hero hype. Many superhero comics advertise clubs that cost $15 to $20 to join. They offer official badges, secret decoders, posters, etc. Most of the children felt that what they received was simply not worth the money spent.

Street marts. The watch was touted as a Rolex, the perfume pure Chanel, and the shirts Ralph Lauren specials. A few weeks after they bought their treasures from street vendors, the children found out that claims were false. The "Rolex" stopped working, the perfume lost its scent and the colors in the shirts ran in the wash. When they went back to complain to the street vendors, they were gone.

What's a Parent to Do When a Child Makes a Mistake?

The conventional answer might be to warn the children of the possibilities of these borderline scams. While that's not a bad thing to do, it rarely works. The best learning tool is disappointment. It lays the groundwork for intense learning. The experience can turn a neophyte buyer into a savvy consumer when punctuated with a few well-timed, sympathetic parental questions:

- Why do you think this happened?
- Can you think of something the vendor said that most appealed to you?
- Do you know why the picture on the ad was so enticing?
- What would you do now before you join another hero club or buy something pictured on a cereal box, advertised on television or hawked by a street vendor?

ACTIVITIES

Talking Back to the Television

Join kids as they watch television, casually talking about the commercials and discussing how they are designed to get people to buy things. This always raises a child's awareness of the subtleties of advertising. If a particular ad runs counter to what a child knows as true, suggest she "talk back." ("Oh, yeah! I tried that and it tasted awful.") Children realize that their opinions are valuable and worth hearing.

Shopping Assistants and Assistance

Kids love to accompany their parents on supermarket jaunts, so capitalize on their enthusiasm by making them your assistants. As the family's assistant shopper, they have specific assignments:

- **The label reader.** Once your child is aware that products list their ingredients in order of the amount used, she'll get a better idea of what's in the food and over-the-counter medications the family eats and uses.

- **The "best-buy" judge.** To determine what the best buy is among the various sizes of the products you use, ask your child to figure out the price per ounce or per pound of each of the sizes. If your child is not old enough to do the computation, do it for her or ask her to read the cost per ounce listed on most supermarket shelves. (Every once in a while there's a big surprise. The giant size is *more* expensive per ounce than the regular size.) The best-buy judge also has to take into consideration whether the family will use the bigger size before it spoils. Also she has to figure out if you have enough room to store the large size. Once she has determined all the factors—price per ounce, if the family will use the large size before it spoils, if there's storage room for it—she'll be able to "advise" you on the purchase.
- **The name-brand determiner.** Sometimes name brands are decidedly better than a generic or store brand because they use different ingredients, use different proportions of the same ingredients, or use a different manner of preparation. But not always. Ask your child to help do some product testing. Once in a while, buy a generic or store brand and ask her to compare it to the brand you usually use. Taste tests are fun and can be made into a family activity.
- **The shopping-list writer.** Have your son or daughter write up the list of what you determine the family needs plus a couple of items he or she would like to add. This curbs much of the impulse spending that occurs when you shop without a clear agenda and prevents a return trip to the store because you forgot something. An unexpected benefit: Kids get so involved in checking off items on the list that they forget to drop unlisted snacks into the cart.

Be an Ad Checker

Kids don't have any idea how many times a day they are bombarded with people telling them what to buy. To raise their consciousness of this ad barrage, have them do an ad check by filling in the following chart while watching television one evening. Give them a watch with a second hand so they can time the commercial.

Show	Name of Product	Length of Ad	What Makes the Ad Special (Clever Phrases, Catchy Jingles)
________	________	________	________
________	________	________	________
________	________	________	________
________	________	________	________

Total time watching television ________

Total time watching commercials ________

What is it about ads that makes you want to buy the product (words, phrases, pictures, music)? ________

What is the ad trying to make you believe, other than that the product is good? ________

Sell Me

Here's an activity that kids can play with each other or with you. Each child makes an item he will try to sell: a greeting card, his own soft drink or cereal concoction, or any craft project. Then she develops a "sales pitch" to sell the group the product. Kids are encouraged to ask questions, try the product, discuss among themselves which they would buy and why, and finally make their individual decisions. Would they or would they not buy the product and why?

Chapter Eight

Sharing and Caring

Moving a Child Beyond the "Me" Stage

Scene: Mother and ten-year-old Gretchen talking.

Gretchen: How come you send grandma $100 a month, but you won't buy me the leather jacket I've been wanting for the past six months?

Your Choice of Responses

You can say:

1. "It's really none of your affair what I send to grandma."
2. "Grandma *needs* the money to pay off her doctor bills. You don't *need* the leather jacket."
3. "We'd certainly like to do both, but since we don't have enough money to help take care of grandma and buy you a leather jacket, we have to make a decision. I feel our first responsibility is to help out family members in need."

A LOOK BEHIND THE RESPONSES

Choice (3) contains all the elements to help a child understand how important familial responsibility is.

Most children will drop change into a box perched on the counter near a cash register if the cause it touts seems even remotely worthwhile. Give them a cause that asks them to participate in a "thon"—telethon, walk-a-thon, dance-a-thon, bike-a-thon, even read-a-thon—and they'll respond with zeal. When schools start a "Feed the Hungry" drive, kids lug cans of food into school. They are moved by the plight of the homeless, other children, animals, and people suffering as a result of a natural disaster. Children are generous and sympathetic by nature.

Because our society so closely associates *giving* with *money*, children sometimes feel frustrated because they don't have large sums to distribute to those in need or to spend on people they love. Our job as parents is to nurture and expand their generosity and empathy and to teach them to use their talents, their time *and* their money in ways they may not have considered.

One to One: The Art of Giving

A four-year-old may want to give her father a toy *she* would like to have, but older children want desperately for the other person to adore the present. They watch closely when the gift is opened and they can be brought to tears if even a flicker of disappointment crosses the loved one's face. Start early in teaching your child the art of gift giving: putting herself in the recipient's place and seeing life from another person's perspective.

When your child is having a hard time deciding what to get someone, ask him to think of the best gift he ever received. Spark his imagination by asking him why it was special. Was it handmade? Was it something he always wanted? Did it belong to someone else previously? Was it from a different country? Did it come in a box or was it another kind of gift? Remind him, too, that gifts don't have to come from a store, that they can be a child's creative endeavors: personal poems, collages, or collections of drawings or photos.

Again, parents who encourage discussion about selecting a present show children, by example, that it's important to think about what you're giving—"Ellen loves animal figurines. I looked at her collection and saw she didn't have anything like the cute kangaroo I saw in the store, so I bought her one for her birthday." Listen to what other people say about their hobbies, interests and likes and dislikes, and give something that will be appreciated.

One mother, who must have set some powerful examples, tells of the best present she ever received. It was from her ten-year-old daughter who had bought a book on foot massaging, learned the techniques and gave her mother, a saleswoman who spends all day on her feet, a birthday present of a foot massage every Friday night for a year.

A twelve-year-old boy and his ten-year-old sister learned, almost by accident, what a meaningful gift is all about. They secretly entered their mother into a Mother's Day "Mother of the Year" contest sponsored by a local newspaper. They composed a letter that told how much they loved, admired and cared about her. However, when it came to giving her the gift—a copy of the letter they had submitted to the paper—they were somewhat apologetic. With glum faces they told her she hadn't won the contest. The mother recalled her words, which she hoped had conveyed the message that their gift was the most meaningful she had ever received. She said, "I have won. Everything I ever wanted is in that letter." She framed it immediately and it sits on her desk where she looks at it daily.

The Art of Receiving

Glee comes naturally from children who open a present they've dreamed of for months. Their spontaneous "thank yous" are so genuine that everyone in the room has to smile.

It's much harder for children to mask disappointment. One eight-year-old who had a difficult time with geography at school received a globe for her birthday from her sister. Her glow disappeared when she realized what she had received. She cried. The birthday girl saw this as a mean trick that reminded her daily of the misery she faced at school. Yet the older sister had specifically chosen this gift because she thought her sister would like spinning the globe and thus learn to enjoy geography.

It would be unfair to expect children to jump for joy after receiving something they don't want or understand the value of. But it is important to help a child find an appropriate way to accept the gift.

First, talk to the child in private about her feelings of disappointment and acknowledge them. They're very real to her.

Second, explain that even though she might not like the gift, the person who gave it had spent money and time getting it. That effort has to be recognized. In addition, help her look for *one* (just one) thing that she thinks is good about the gift. "Red is my favorite color," even though a jar of red-hot candy is the last thing she wanted for Christmas. Or "this sweater fits very well," even though she would never wear an orange sweater if it was freezing and that was the only sweater she owned.

Perfectly acceptable ways of asking about returning a gift can be practiced by the child beforehand: "This baseball glove is really great. It's too bad I have one like it. Is it possible to return it for some other piece of sports equipment?" "Orange is a great color for most people and I wish I looked good in it. Is it possible to return the sweater for a different color?"

Acknowledging gifts given by people who are not there when the gift is opened means a child has to phone or write her thanks—something many children recoil from. Either they "don't really know Aunt Sally, so what should I say to her on the phone?" or they "don't know what to write." So they procrastinate. Prodding a child to acknowledge a present is like prodding her to clean her room: It's necessary and sooner or later you hope it will become habit.

GENEROUS TO A FAULT

It is difficult to pinpoint exactly when giving valuable commodities—time, money, things—turns into a problem, but we do know that when a child uses gifts to buy or compete for affection, attention or love, something must be done. Generally "overgenerosity" results for one of three reasons:

1. A child has a great need for approval and friendship. He offers his things as a way to get another child to play with him or to like him. Often other kids sense this need and manipulate the needy child by saying "I'll be your friend if you give me your money (game, food)." To fill the approval gap, extra attention from a parent may be needed.

2. A child has a great need for control. He will give to (or take back from) another child material objects or money. Sometimes the transaction appears to be in the form of a loan. ("You can wear my watch today if you let me be the pitcher in our game.") Other times it's in the form of a threat. ("Give me back my watch. I'm giving it to Alan. He does what I want and you don't.") Children act this way often because they feel powerless in a home environment. Granting this child more decision-making authority at home may help, especially in areas that affect him directly, such as picking out the paint color for his room or being allowed to decorate it as he'd like.

3. The child is extremely competitive in a materialistic sense. He feels he must outdo everyone else and will often give the best gift at birthday parties or a lavish present to the teacher at the end of the year. Some of these children place special value on material items. They may equate giving the best gift with being the best child. Parents need to reassure such children that they are loved and praised for what they are, not what they give. And examine the behavior in the home. If a child hears mom or dad crowing about the expensive gift they have just given (or received), the child will assume that only expensive gifts please people.

Don't be concerned if your child has an occasional spurt of overgenerosity. Most do and require no parental attention. Occasionally, you'll have to point out that friendship cannot be bought or sold and that the best gifts are those involving time and thought. That should be enough to shove him through the overly generous stage unscathed. If the excessive generosity is ongoing and grossly inappropriate, however, it may signal that he has some deeper concerns about himself and may require professional therapy.

THE MISERY OF THE MISER

We know that only a "y" separates miser from misery and we cringe at the thought that the child who won't share his possessions with friends or family might become both miser and miserable.

Children have to *learn* to share and spend on others (see chapter two, "While They're Still Tots"). These aren't natural behaviors. But shouldn't they have learned these skills by the time they're into their school years? Sometimes.

Consider the generation that came to age in the 1930s and early 1940s—our own parents perhaps. The hoarding of money and possessions that is so much a part of a "depression mentality" was born of deprivation. They feared that hard economic times might be around the corner and they didn't want to be unprepared—again. People who have experienced a physical deprivation early in life find that changing their behavior is difficult even though circumstances may have changed. On a less dramatic scale, that principle can also hold true if children are deprived of ownership or control as they grow. Youngsters need to feel some things are theirs and under their control. (Another reason why an allowance is a good idea.)

On a psychological level, children who feel insecure or unloved may hold onto things (money, possessions) as if they were the comfortable, tattered security blankets of their toddler years. Sharing may mean giving up the source of security and comfort that are now represented by material possessions. When children feel more secure, they begin to test their sharing skills.

RAISING CONSCIOUSNESS: TEACHING BY EXAMPLE

Dr. Benjamin Spock wrote, "I think that more of our children would grow up happier and more stable if they were acquiring a conviction, all through childhood, that the most important and most fulfilling thing human beings can do is to serve humanity in some fashion and to live by their ideals." Of course, he adds, "this does not preclude their earning a living or seeking advancement."

Children overhear and listen to parents. If parents talk about concerns and problems in the neighborhoods, country and the world at large, they raise the social consciousness of children—without even trying!

And kids love the family tales. Over and over they ask to hear about the one where grandpa helped save a stranger who was almost run over by a bus or about a great grandmother who used to feed all the children on the block. The tales we choose to tell our children reflect who we are as a family and what we value.

Although talk is very important, learning by example is a more powerful instructor.

Children should be aware of our efforts to be part of the solutions, whether we're members of the local Lions Club that raises money for worthy projects in the community, active in the political system, or simply, but equally important, the dinner-bearers for a bedridden neighbor. Our genuine enthusiasm for doing these things is contagious. Common sense and research indicate that children with involved parents will be more predisposed to this type of prosocial behavior later in their lives.

Just as we join others in striving to make the world a better place to live, children should be encouraged to do the same. Youth groups affiliated with religious organizations, scouting groups, school classrooms that interact with their communities through such projects as food drives offer children this opportunity.

Family Service

Giving to the community or to people in need within the community *as a family* is a powerful learning experience.

"One of the highlights of my life as a parent and as a member of our community was when about fifty of us—parents and children—worked side by side one weekend putting together a tire park," says one father whose two children are now young adults. "The playground equipment consisted of used, donated tires, imaginatively designed by a well-known park architect. Instead of hiring a construction crew, families volunteered and assembled the tires according to the architect's specifications. We were so exhausted after it was finished—but so proud. Even today, my twenty-five-year-old son will drive past the active sixteen-year-old park and say, 'Dad, there's our playground. Wasn't that a wonderful weekend. I want to do something like that with my children—when I have them.' "

Another family emphasizes the "thanks" in Thanksgiving Day by having their traditional dinner on Wednesday night and spending Thursday delivering "Meals on Wheels" to shut-ins. "When one of the homebound recipients touched my eight-year-old son and said 'Thank you. I didn't think I would be eating anything today,' tears sprang to his eyes," the father says. "Mine too. When we came out of the apartment, my son turned to me and said, 'I'm so glad we do this.' Then a few seconds later he added, 'We're really so lucky.' " Volunteer opportunities for children exist in great number. For more information, read *What Would We Do Without You? A Guide to Volunteer Activities for Kids* (Betterway Books).

Do as I Do

Kids may grow up disagreeing with their parents politically, even religiously. But it's very difficult to shake off the values of sharing and giving and caring that they are exposed to as they grow. Saying one thing ("We feel so badly about Aunt Edna's injuries . . .") and doing another (". . . but we can't visit her or help her because we're just too busy.") confuses them: It opens their eyes to the hypocrisy of their parents' views; at worst, it teaches them that providing lip service in place of real service is just fine. The rules we set down for children in the areas of charity and giving are not nearly as important as providing them with strong role models.

ACTIVITIES

"I Am the Gift" Gift

The gift of time and consideration is the most precious gift of all, and as one gets older its influence extends beyond the scope of family and friends and into the community at large. Encourage children to give "Personal: What I Will Do for You" coupons for holidays or birthdays—gifts that are matched to the recipient's needs, interests or passions. Children can:

- Serve breakfast in bed every Saturday morning in August (for a working mom).
- Take two rolls of film of someone's cat and give that person an 8″ × 10″ of the best picture (for a cat aficionado).
- Let someone wear their best sweater—the one that person has always wanted to borrow—four times this winter (for a younger sister from an older one).
- Clean the basement (from any youngster to anybody with a basement who doesn't like to or can't clean it).
- Designed by the child on a 3″ × 5″ card, the "What I Will Do for You" gift coupons should include this information:

To:
From:
I Promise to ______________________________
____
Expires ______________________________
(The expiration date is to ensure that the child doesn't forget to fulfill his gift coupon promise.)

Creative Thank-You Notes

If your child is stuck in the "what do I say" rut when it comes to thank-you notes, urge a little creativity. If he draws well, perhaps he can draw his reaction to the gift or a picture of how he looks using or wearing the present. If he's a budding poet, the thank you note can be in verse.

Because saying thank you in writing for a gift that is somewhat less than perfect is often easier than trying to come up with the right words on the phone, encourage disappointed young recipients to think of the best thing about the present (i.e., it fits) and focus the short thank-you note on that:

Dear Uncle Henry,
The cap and gloves you sent me fit perfectly. I bet I'll never be cold when I have them on and I'm playing in the snow. Thank you very much for your generosity. Maybe we will see you soon.

If there's no best thing, then suggest your child concentrate on the generosity or the thoughtfulness of the gift-giver and emphasize that in writing.

Dear Uncle Henry,
You always remember to send me a Christmas gift and I'm touched by your thoughtfulness. Maybe next year we'll celebrate the holidays together—that will be the best gift of all.
Thank you and happy holiday.

Sharing the Sharing

Let children be part of your charitable activities as early as possible. For example, when they're little, they can tell you which toys they no longer play with and which clothes are too small and then you take these items to a shelter for homeless families or other charitable organization. When they're older, they can come with you and spend a few moments playing with some of the children there. Share the experience and talk about it afterward. The lasting effect comes when children understand that there are situations and conditions outside of ourselves and our families that are also important and worthy of our time and money.

The Three Wishes

Here's a thinking game that works especially well when you're cooped up in a car. "What would you wish for if you were given three wishes?" almost always nets one response like "all the money in the world," "a zillion dollars" or "winning the lottery." Sounds good to children, of course, until you explore with them what that would mean. Questions such as "What happens to other people if you had all the money in the world?", "How would you spend your huge wealth?" and "How would the money affect your relationship with your friends?" help them gain insight into the pluses and minuses of great wealth and the reponsibilities that accompany it.

Chapter Nine

Choices

Big Problems for Small Folks

Scene: Father and nine-year-old Dennis looking down at the floor where the pieces of a shattered vase and flowers lay in a pool of water.

Father: I've told you a hundred times not to play ball in the house. What do I have to do to you to make you understand?

Your Choice of Responses

You can:

1. Ground Dennis for a week.
2. Take away his ball.
3. Make him clean up the broken vase.
4. Make him pay for another vase.

A LOOK BEHIND THE RESPONSES

Accidents happen, but this one was clearly preventable had Dennis followed house rules. Dennis should be responsible for cleaning up the breakage (3) and, in part or entirely depending on his age and the cost of the vase, be responsible for replacing it at his expense (4) or doing extra work around the house—work he would normally get paid for—to cover the cost of a new vase. Taking away his ball (2) provides some connection between action and consequence; but since the ball isn't going to be out of his life forever, a time limit on the punishment is needed. Grounding him (1) is not terribly effective in fostering responsibility, but it isn't a harmful action for an exasperated parent to take.

PROVIDING GUIDANCE

Growing up is a struggle—children have to learn to make hard decisions, suffer the consequences of many mistakes and grapple with issues of morality and ethics that crop up in everyday events (even if they don't know that's what they're doing). Not that adults don't have similar struggles. We do. But by the time we reach this stage of our lives, some of the basic issues have been thought through and settled, many mistakes have been made and learned from, and a fairly defined set of values and principles automatically guides much of our decision making.

In this chapter we'll look at the money-related, moral-testing situations and scrapes even great kids (with loving, caring, responsible parents) find themselves in regularly. We'll also examine the parent's role as they provide children with needed guidance.

Things Borrowed, Broken, Damaged or Taken

Kids lend each other nickels, dimes and quarters all the time. As they move out of the piggy-bank stage, most don't give much thought to coin change; they don't even consider it "real" money. But they do remember dollars they lend to each other. (Memory is not quite as sharp when it comes to money they borrow!) When the money exchange becomes unequal, problems develop.

A child lends money to another, but the borrower won't or can't repay it. Let's assume the borrower is our own child who, overcome with desire to spend the day with the other kids at an amusement park, asks a friend if he can borrow money for the day, which he will pay back.

Sometimes kids hope they'll find the money somewhere; other times they know full well there's no way they can repay the loan, but the lure of the event or the thing overwhelms them.

Frequently, we hear about our child's dilemma first from the injured lender who, after trying to collect his due from our child, takes his case to a higher court—the debtor's parents. Obviously, the story has to be checked out, privately, with our own child. Once its accuracy is established, the lessons begin. The fact that the errant debt is now public knowledge oils the learning experience. No child likes to be embarrassed.

Parent's Responsibility: People or institutions lending us money on good faith have every right to expect that it will be returned. If our son's friend wants or needs the whole sum back right now and can't accept an installment method of repayment, we can advance our child the money to pay off his loan (he should be the one to physically hand over the money) *and* make a new contract with our child so that he now has a financial commitment to us. Whatever repayment is agreed on—from allowance, earnings, money from gifts or work—the loan must be repaid to us. If not, we encourage an irresponsible "spend now, pay never" mindset.

Just as money changes hands often among children, so do things. That presents opportunity for mishaps.

A youngster lends someone something that is never returned. Suppose your child was the magnanimous one and let her friend have her favorite doll for the night. Come morning the friend refuses to give it back and your daughter comes to you in tears.

Parent's Responsibility: We provide sympathetic listening, ask probing questions, work with our child to develop a solid gameplan to retrieve the object and help her draw some lessons from the experience.

Everyone needs to pour out a sad story, and having a favorite doll snatched from you by a friend is a very sad tale for a six-year-old. So parents should be there to listen empathetically. Too, questions should be asked about why the friend is holding onto the doll. Is she sick? Does she want it only until she feels better? Is the doll the only plaything she has ever seen? Has she taken things and not returned them before?

If we determine that there's no real reason for the doll not to be returned promptly, we must help our child develop a plan to get it back. It may be that she'll speak to her friend's parents about the problem. If she does, she'll need help in framing her plea in a way that will draw the parents into the solution, such as "Is there anything you can do to help me get my doll back?" To be effective in this grown-up approach, she'll need to practice. Be there to listen and to coach. If she is not successful with the parents, we have to step in and meet with the friend's parents. Clearly, children need role models for how to approach and solve problems and they need to know that when something is important to us, we have a right and a responsibility to stand up for it.

What if that same doll is not returned because our daughter's friend's dog chewed it into bits? That changes the picture somewhat because the breach is not willful. While we would hope that the friend (and her parents) would feel responsible for the doll and give our daughter money to replace it, that might not always be possible. Sometimes the family doesn't have the money. But even if they did, our daughter might have a special attachment to the doll that is irreplaceable. Understanding her loss may not make her feel better at the moment, but it may help her deal with the idea that accidents happen and blame doesn't always have to be placed.

Careless or negligent behavior causes a loss of something valuable. A child uses our computer to play games. One night he takes a soda with him and it accidentally spills onto the keyboard. The next morning we turn on the computer and find that it's not working properly. We check it out and find that the soda spill had caused the damage and we have to buy a new keyboard.

Parent's Responsibility: Unless children are specifically instructed how to use and care for a piece of equipment (or anything else for that matter), they can't be expected to know, so punishing them for an accident at this stage is unfair. As parents, our first responsibility is to teach proper use and care. If the steps involved are complicated or numerous, we can develop a checklist and keep it close to the item. For example, when it comes to the computer, we might attach a card below the screen entitled "Directions for Using."

Suppose we do all that and the child still puts his soda down on the desk right near the keyboard. Since rights and responsibilities are interrelated, one appropriate stance is to take away the right to use the computer. If the child's continuing negligence results in damage to the computer, it is fair to require that the child pay for the repair.

Malicious mischief causes damage to property. It's Halloween night and a group of kids pelt a neighbor's house with eggs. The neighbor tracks down the culprits and calls the parents. We're surprised that we are called. When confronted, our child squirms, denies but finally admits it.

Parent's Responsibility: Of course, our child will have to make restitution, and in the egg-pelting scenario it will probably be spending whatever time (and money) it takes to clean off the egg splatter from the neighbor's house. But probably no more powerful learning experience occurs than when the accused has to come face-to-face with the accuser and hear about the damage or the hurt he has caused. So insist the child make a face-to-face apology (rather than just taking care of the damage while the neighbor is away at work). This underscores the realization that a real person was injured by this kids-will-be-kids escapade.

A youngster takes something from a friend's house without asking. "Thing-lifting," such as taking without permission five pens from a friend's mother's desk or a pocketful of M&Ms from a bowl in a friend's house is common among children, mainly because they don't think of thing-lifting as a big deal. Because the things are usually small and of little value, kids rarely equate taking them with stealing (an act most children have been taught is wrong).

Parent's Responsibility: Even the strictest parents know that this type of impropriety is bound to happen. (Chances are they thing-lifted when they were kids, as well.) Still, children must be taught that anything you take from another without its being granted freely is stealing. The best antidote to preventing thing-lifting from becoming an ongoing problem is to get caught.

If you're pretty sure that your child has stolen something, be firm about wanting to know where and how she got it. Don't make it easy to wiggle out of the truth. If you do, it appears as if you're condoning the theft. Once caught, children should know their parents disapprove of what they did (not that the parents don't love them) and the parents should insist on immediate restitution. This presents parents with an opportunity to communicate values.

One twenty-year-old tells of the last time she ever took anything from anyone else. "I was in the doctor's waiting room and there was a big brandy snifter full of hundreds of plastic charms—with a sign reading 'Take one on your way out.' In my community every girl between the ages of eight and fifteen was collecting these gold-painted animals and figures. When no one was looking, I stuck my hand in and pocketed a fistful of them. I wasn't good at covering up transgressions even then, but I did fend off my mother's 'What's wrong?' queries fairly well until she found the charms in my dresser drawer and knew immediately what had happened. She took it very seriously and made me phone the doctor to make an appointment with him so I could return the charms and apologize. I had no choice in the matter. I honestly can't remember what he said—though I'm sure he was nice enough about it—but I do remember thinking that the momentary delight of the charms wasn't worth the mortification of owning up to the theft. Years later, when I recalled the story to my mother, she admitted, 'I never thought it was a big deal. But I wanted you to think it was. So I called the doctor before you went over and we cooked up the script we were going to use to deal with the situation. I'm glad it worked.' "

A youngster takes something from a store without paying. Shoplifting is one step beyond "thing-lifting"—and a bit more distant, because kids take things from faceless, nameless institutions. Even kids of conscientious parents do it—once, twice or more—until they get caught or until they outgrow the daring "fun" of getting away with something.

Parent's Responsibility: Immediately confront a child once the incident has been discovered. It's not that the child will turn into a hardened criminal if not challenged, but rather this presents a situation that directly links values to behavior and allows us to talk to our school-age children about the larger, ethical issues. Obviously, the child must return, replace or pay back the stolen items. Again, insisting on face-to-face apologies helps the child understand that thefts affect people—store owners and employees. Many parents will also want their children to understand their own displeasure with the theft by imposing some other form of discipline, such as grounding the child for a week.

One preventative measure parents can take is to monitor—without snooping—children's possessions. If a nine-year-old has a compact disc the parents have never seen before, the parents have the right to ask about it, even to ask to see the receipt, if the explanation seems fishy.

If the shoplifting appears to have some underlying psychological causes or is compulsive and continuous in nature, then professional therapeutic help should be sought.

Flaunting, Pressure, Jealousy and Fright

A youngster constantly lauds her possessions and her money over her peers. Kids will flaunt things every now and again. But when it happens constantly, it might mean that the child's self-image needs shoring up. She might think that she's not important enough by herself; that she needs to parade out her things to get people to care for her. Another explanation for excessive flaunting might be that she hears her parents say "My car's bigger/better/more expensive than the neighbor's." Flaunting then is a learned trait.

Parent's Responsibility: Forget about the occasional flaunt. If, however, your child regularly flashes around her possessions, search for reasons.

If we can help her understand that her popularity rests not on what she has but on who she is, we can help her bolster her self-confidence. While her fears about herself and her relationship to her peers may seem ill-founded—perhaps silly—to us, they're real to her. Perhaps we can talk about what she does well and how she can use those traits to develop the socialization skills she may feel she lacks. It helps to have her practice her response to those situations she most fears.

Also we must examine our own family's reaction to new things or things of value. Do we spend an inordinate amount of time discussing them, taking pride in them, glorifying them? If so, we can't be surprised if our children do the same.

Peers pressure a child to spend more than he has, more than he wants to spend. Children measure themselves against their friends. Being different means risking disapproval from the very group from whom approval is all-meaningful. Even though saying "no" or "I can't" or "I don't have" rarely results in a child being dropped from his friends' social register, many kids aren't secure enough to take the chance of not going along with friends.

Parent's Responsibility: Friends are important, sometimes all-important depending on the stage of our child's life. If a child can't keep pace with his circle of spenders, we must help him understand his options. He could earn extra spending money, which has two advantages. First, he doesn't miss out on most of the fun because he has the extra money he needs. Second, while he's earning the money, he doesn't have the time to spend it.

If his income still cannot keep pace with his fast-spending friends, he might have to start looking for other friends whose choice of activities isn't as costly.

Jealousy over what others have consumes your child. Jealousy and envy are normal and psychologists tell us that they reflect a child's growth. But jealousy and envy are not alike. A jealous child will see another child's Nintendo game and want to take it away from his friend. An envious child will see the game and want one just like it.

While there are many reasons for jealousy in children—sibling rivalry, the need for attention and love—continuous jealousy can be a monster. In its most intense state, it can lead to severe behavioral problems, such as stealing.

Parent's Responsibility: If a child is jealous of what a sibling gets, we have to examine our own behavior. Are we spending more time, more money or more energy on one child over another? Are there unusual circumstances that make that necessary or are we playing favorites? In either case, if a child seems particularly jealous of a sibling, talk about it with him and see if he can tell you what he is feeling. Without giving in to any outrageous demands, the situation often can be righted simply by spending a little private time with the child each week or giving him the extra hug and support you think he needs to feel good about himself.

If jealousy results in a child's stealing, hitting or other negative behavior, we first must disapprove of the act (not of the child!) and then insist he take responsibility for it, such as making restitution for anything stolen, apologize to the person who was hit, etc.

When jealousy is intense and continuous, it can be a sign of emotional distress that requires the help of a therapist.

A child becomes frightened when a parent loses a job or there is a financial crisis in the family. Children are quick to pick up household tension. When no one stops to explain to them what is going on, they become terribly anxious. They don't know whether they are the cause of the stressful household. Even if they sense that isn't the case, that the problems somehow have to do with money, they worry about being like the people they see on television or on the street—homeless. They also worry about things that may be far from true—that their parents are going to divorce, that someone's going to die, that they're going to move far away from their friends.

Parent's Responsibility: We must explain the financial problem clearly and simply to our children, so that their imaginations don't make a difficult situation a tragic one. The ages and maturity levels of the children will be the clue as to the depth of the conversation. So will the questions they ask. The following explanation for putting off a purchase states the problem, removes the fear, offers a solution and fosters discussion.

"The company I work for is trying to save money, so it's not giving any bonuses this year. We were counting on that extra money to get a new car in October, but since we won't receive the bonus, we'll keep this car for a year until we've saved the money we need for a downpayment on a new one."

While kids will often be willing to make sacrifices to help in a financial bind ("You can use the money I'm saving for the car."), we mustn't let children feel responsible for solving the financial difficulties. That's in the grown-up's domain.

GUIDING PRINCIPLES

As kids grapple with issues and situations that seem overwhelming to them, we parents can follow three major principles.

1. Let the children know that making a mistake or having a problem is not a disgrace and that love is not going to be withheld because of it. Talking openly about mistakes enhances trust, understanding, and the child's self esteem.
2. Discuss how to keep an error from recurring. Be sure children understand what went wrong and what they can do so it doesn't happen again.
3. Explore options and pave the way for children to become

problem-solvers. Help them understand that while many situations are not clear-cut, there are certain principles and values the family holds dear that can help when they're trying to decide what to do and why.

ACTIVITIES

Hard Choice Cards

Write the following "Hard Choices" on 3″ × 5″ index cards, one situation per card, and tuck them into the glove compartment of your car. When you're on a long trip or when the kids seem bored and need something to do, pull them out and use them as the basis for a family discussion (not lecture). They allow you to talk about difficult ethical and moral situations in a safe, relaxed setting. Give the children plenty of time to voice their own responses and to ask each other and you questions.

1. Two months ago your friend borrowed $10 from you for a birthday gift for his mother. About a week later, he paid you back. He forgets about the repayment and now hands you another $10 and thanks you for lending him the money for the gift.

What would you do?

---

2. You lend a friend $5 for a movie because she forgot her wallet. She says she'll pay you back as soon as you get home. She doesn't pay you then, nor does she make any move to pay you back in the weeks to come.

What would you do?

---

3. You remind your friend that he owes you $5 which he borrowed last week. Instead of paying it back, as he promised, he gets angry and tells you to stop bugging him or you'll never get the money.

What would you do?

---

4. As a way of making money for yourself, you sell flower seeds to neighbors. One of your customers gives you the $5 he owes for the seeds. After you get home you notice there's another $5 stuck to the original bill.

What would you do?

Would your decision be any different if you were selling the seeds for a charity?

---

5. You just bought a great video game and on the way home you dropped it by mistake. When you got home and unwrapped it, you noticed the plastic casing was cracked, which made it impossible to insert into the video.

What would you do?

---

6. You're riding your bike without really thinking about where you're going and you crack it into a neighbor's parked car. Your bike is slightly damaged, and the neighbor's car is scratched. You don't think anyone saw the accident.

What would you do?

---

7. You buy an ice cream cone for $1.25 and hand the clerk a $5 bill. By mistake, the clerk gives you $8.75 in change.

What would you do?

If the clerk had been rude and nasty to you, would that influence your decision about what to do?

---

8. You make a call from a pay telephone to tell mom you're staying for an after-school activity. You misdial, punch the coin return, and all of a sudden what seems like a hundred coins come pouring out of the slot.

What would you do?

---

9. One of your brother's friends has a job as cashier at the local grocery. Every time you go in to get something, he either waves you past so you pay nothing or he rings up only some of the items you purchase (though he packs all of them).

What would you do?

10. On the street, you find a handbag with $400 in it, along with a watch and some credit cards.

What would you do?

What would you do if the handbag only had money and no identification in it?

---

11. There's an amusement park that gives a discount to people under the age of eight. You're eleven but you could pass for eight.

What would you do?

---

12. For your birthday, your grandparents have told you to get yourself a pair of sneakers of your choosing, which they will pay for as long as the price doesn't exceed $75. You shop around and find the pair you want costs $39.95. You see another pair of shoes you like for $32. If you buy them also, you're still under the $75 limit.

What would you do?

---

13. You lost your new watch and your parents give you $25 to buy another just like it. Just as you're about to enter the watch store, you discover the "lost" one deep inside your pocket.

What would you do?

---

14. You and your friend both mow lawns for extra money. So that you aren't fighting for the same customers you make a deal. Everyone on one side of the street is your potential customer. Everyone on the other side of the street is his potential customer. Your parents' best friends move in on his side of the street.

What would you do?

---

15. You're babysitting for a neighbor's three-year-old who opens her piggy bank and shows you how much money she has. She hands you two dollar bills and says she wants you to have them.

What would you do?

16. Your parents give you a $20 bill and ask you to stop at the supermarket to get milk, margarine and ketchup. You get home and put everything in the refrigerator.

What do you do with the change?

---

17. You have $123 saved for a bike. A friend of yours is selling hers for $100. It's not in bad condition but it has dents and nicks. The bike you really want is $320. You figure you need about five more months to save up for it.

What would you do?

What would influence your decision?

---

18. You see a friend take money out of another friend's pocket. You have no idea if he's stealing or if he had the friend's permission to take out the money.

What would you do?

---

19. You are taking a shortcut through your neighbor's yard (even though you're not supposed to) and accidentally knock over some clay pots, which break into hundreds of pieces.

What would you do?

Would you do anything differently if the pots were expensive china pots instead of inexpensive clay ones?

---

20. Your mother and father are divorced and they don't speak to each other. Your mother tells you to ask your father for half the money for a class trip. She says if he doesn't give it to you, then she'll pay for the whole thing. You ask your father for half and he gives it to you.

What do you tell your mother?

---

21. You entered yourself into a walk-a-thon for charity and collected $43 from your sponsors, which you sent into the charity.

Your grandparents come over and hand you $10 for your efforts. You assume they are giving it to the charity, but they haven't made that absolutely clear.

What would you do?

---

22. Your friend, an excellent artist, told you that she would tie-dye a T-shirt for you for your birthday. Your birthday has come and gone and she never gave you the shirt.

What would you do?

---

23. You have a Nintendo video game that you're tired of and that your friend is eager to have. He's offered to trade you some of the stamps in his father's stamp collection for it. Because you're a collector and he isn't, you know that the value of the stamps is about three times the value of the video game. You aren't sure if your friend's father knows about this arrangement.

What would you do?

Chapter Ten

Concerns

Questions Kids Ask . . . With Good Answers

Scene: Dad in den working on income tax return. Six-year-old George enters.

George: "What are you doing, Dad?"

Dad: "Our income taxes."

George: "What's that?"

Your Choice of Responses

You can:

1. Say, "I'm busy, George. Don't bother me."
2. Say, "You're too young to understand. I'll explain when you're older."
3. Stop what you're doing and explain what goes into the 1040 form.
4. Give a simple explanation of income tax, appropriate to the level of understanding of a six-year-old.

A LOOK BEHIND THE RESPONSES

Choice (4) has the right elements, although you might explain that you're busy now and that you'll explain it a little later. As long as the child seems genuinely interested, he deserves an answer in terms he'll understand. But trying to overdo the response by explaining every detail of the form will bore him and might leave him hesitant to ask questions in the future.

CURIOSITY AND LEARNING

Questions, children's most effective learning tools, make perfect teaching opportunities. Our challenge as parents is to capitalize on our children's natural curiosity by answering the questions simply and honestly. No small feat when they ask questions that revolve around difficult and complicated economic or philosophical concepts.

The younger child will often ask the "technical" money questions; the older one will ask more probing, theoretical ones. What follows are questions that have been posed to us when we talked with groups of children ages eight to eleven and the uncomplicated answers that left them satisfied they had learned something. (We're assuming that you, the parent, are answering the question.)

ABOUT MONEY

Who first discovered money? We don't really know. Money was probably "discovered" or "invented" by different people in different parts of the world. Probably a group of people agreed on items that could be used to trade or exchange for other items or services. Certain shells were once used as money. A coconut might cost three shells; a fish, eight shells. And you know from school that the Indians used beads (wampum) for money.

What did people do before money? Trading and bartering happened long ago, not too different from what you do now when you trade comic books for baseball cards. But way back before money, people would trade an animal fur for some arrows, some fruit for a bead necklace, the services of a healer for handmade shoes.

Why did we start using coins and paper money? The "money" different groups were using had certain limitations—fish rotted, shells broke, animal hides were large and too bulky to carry easily. People began to realize that the best "money" was small, easy to use, strong, and not too difficult to make. Coins were the first answer to the challenge. Some historians think the first people to use coins were the people of Mesopotamia (an ancient land where Iraq and Syria are located today) perhaps five thousand years ago. Others think it was the Egyptians about forty-five hundred years ago.

However, when people had a lot of money, they found that carrying the coins was heavy. Too heavy. The governments decided to make some money from paper so it would be easier to carry.

How did people decide how much each coin would be worth? At first, coins were weighed to decide how much they were worth. Later (and now) they were minted, which means that each coin is made to a uniform size and shape and a design is stamped on it. People agreed that one design would be worth more or less than another. (Take out coins and talk about how much more a nickel is worth than a penny, a quarter than a nickel and so on.)

How is our money made? Paper money is printed at the U.S. Bureau of Engraving and Printing in Washington, D.C. In order to prevent counterfeiting—when someone other than the government makes money, an illegal act—the government uses:

- Special paper made of linen and cotton. It is illegal for anyone else to make this paper without special permission.
- A secret formula ink.
- Special plates to print the designs on bills.

These plates are very difficult to copy exactly. (Children who have done linoleum block printing or potato printing can immediately see the similarity between that kind of printing and the engraving process.)

All our coins are made at the U.S. Government Mint. (Not a flavor, but a place.) If you look right under George Washington's ponytail on the quarter, you'll see a letter. That letter stands for the city in which the coin was minted: D = Denver, O = New Orleans, P = Philadelphia, S = San Francisco.

Coins are made of alloys, mixtures of different metals. Pennies are made of copper and zinc. All other U.S. coins are made of copper and nickel. The alloys are rolled into sheets. Round coin blanks—the size of real coins—are punched out in much the same way a cookie cutter punches out a cookie shape from a sheet of dough. Then machines stamp designs on each side of the coin. The coin is now "real money."

Why is a nickel bigger than a dime? (A good question that really asks why the value of a coin doesn't necessarily relate to its size.) There's no real answer. Long ago people in the United States decided that a nickel would be worth five pennies and a dime would be worth ten pennies. They also decided on the size of each coin and though it may sound illogical (and it is), they decided that size doesn't determine value. Value is determined by common agreement, not unlike a group of children determining that one Dave Winfield baseball card is worth two cards of any other Toronto Blue Jays player.

Why are there different serial numbers on dollar bills? Just as you keep track of where you are in a book by the number on a page, that's how the government can keep track of the bills it prints by having serial numbers. The serial numbers also help catch counterfeiters who make many bills with the same serial numbers.

Why do presidents get their pictures on bills? Though it seems that only presidents (and then, only *some* presidents) have their faces engraved on bills, that's not true. Alexander Hamilton ($10) and Benjamin Franklin ($100) are two of our early leaders who were not presidents. The government can issue new designs with new faces at any time, but it tends not to make such changes once a face has been decided upon. It would be confusing to the public to keep changing pictures. Most of the people pictured on paper money are from America's early history. In fact, all the bills used today are the same in design and size as they were in 1929.

Coins, too, have pictures of people. Abraham Lincoln is on the penny; Thomas Jefferson is on the nickel; Franklin Delano Roosevelt is on the dime; George Washington is on the quarter; and John Kennedy is on the half dollar. (But there aren't many half dollars in circulation.)

Why don't we have more denominations of paper money? We currently have bills of $1, $2 (not frequently seen or used), $5, $10, $20, $50 and $100.

We don't need vast numbers of denominations because it gets confusing for people to use and expensive for the government to make. We can add the denominations we have to make just about any sum we need. If you need $448, for example, you can use four $100s, two $20s, one $5, and three $1s.

Why can't just anyone make money? The most important reason is that it's illegal. But think about what would happen if everyone printed his or her own money. Everyone's money would look different and there wouldn't be any way to judge its worth. And what would happen if people stopped working and just printed up money? Fewer goods would be made (televisions, socks, toys, snacks, etc.) and there would be fewer people performing services (policing, doctoring, apple picking, etc.). That would make the goods on the market and the services performed very expensive. You might have to bring a wheelbarrow of paper money to the store just to buy a loaf of bread that might cost $5,000. Then money would become almost worthless and we might have to return to bartering again.

Why do prices go up and down? Suppose two friends want to buy the same toy from you. Because they both want it, they begin to bid for it, upping the price each time. One friend, Mark, says he'll pay you $6.00 for it; another friend, Susan, says she'll pay you $6.75. Then Mark says he'll give you $7.00 and Susan counters with $7.25. When people want something, they're willing to pay more money for it. Things also cost more money when there isn't enough of an item to go around. So if your sister had the same toy as you had, Mark and Susan each might be able to buy the toy for $6, if both you and your sister were willing to sell. They wouldn't have to bid against each other for one toy. (The concept of supply and demand can be explained early on; the terminology needn't be introduced into a child's vocabulary until later—perhaps around age ten).

Why aren't other natural resources more important to our survival, such as water and soil, worth more than gold and silver? Certainly soil and water have a greater value in terms of human survival. But value and price aren't always the same. Gold and silver have a high price and are costly because they are rarer than water and soil. They also look pretty and shiny when made into jewelry. Traditionally people have been willing to pay high prices for them—especially gold.

ABOUT STOCKS AND BONDS

What are stocks? Stocks are shares in a company. Shares come from sharing. If, for example, five children each chipped in $1 to start a lemonade stand, collectively they would have $5 to buy the pitcher, paper cups, lemons and sugar. They would be partners and each child would own one-fifth (or 20 percent) of the business. If they made $10 selling lemonade for the day, each of them would get back $2 ($1 would represent their original investment and $1 would be profit).

Suppose there were only four children and one put in $2 while the other three put in $1. The first child has two shares to everyone else's one share. After making $10 selling lemonade, she would get back $4 as compared to everyone else's $2.

In big business, people buy shares in a company. You become part owner of the company. You receive a stock certificate telling you how many shares you own.

Why do stocks go up and down in price? Nobody really knows that answer, but usually when a company is doing well and making a profit, the price of its shares goes up. If a company does poorly or has a loss, usually the price of the shares goes down.

But there are other factors too. Even if a company is doing well, something can happen to make people *think* the company won't do well in the future. Suppose the Zippy Zipper Company is doing well making the metal zippers that other companies use when they make jackets. One day, another company announces it has an invention called Velcro, which will replace zippers. People who own shares in the Zippy Zipper Company might think that one day no one will buy zippers anymore. So they try to sell their shares. Other people, reading the same announcement, agree and don't want to buy the shares that are on sale. What will happen? The demand for the shares in the company has gone down and the supply of shares has gone up. When that happens the price of the stock will go down.

What are bonds? When a company or the government needs money (to build new factories or subways, for example), it issues bonds. These bonds are sold to the public and other institutions. If you buy a bond, you're really lending money to a company or to a government. In return, the company or government promises to repay you the principal (the amount you lent), usually five or more years after the bond is issued, and the annual interest (a percentage of the principal). You don't become the company's partner as you do if you're a shareholder. You're more like a banker lending money to a customer.

ABOUT BANKS, LOANS, CREDIT CARDS

What does a bank do with the money you put in it? Surprise! The bank uses your money to make investments and to lend money to people and companies. (Of course, banks must also keep some money in reserve so they don't run out of cash when someone comes in to withdraw money.) But how do they get money to pay you interest if you have a savings account? They charge interest to people who borrow money from them.

So interest works two ways. It's what the bank pays its depositors for allowing their money to be used. It's also what borrowers pay for using the money. Because borrowers pay more interest than depositors get paid, there is money left over. That's the money the bank uses for expenses and for profit.

Suppose, for example, you deposit $10 in a bank and are told you'll get a 5 percent interest return on your money. The bank then takes that money and lends it to a construction company, charging 10 percent interest. At the end of the year, you, the depositor, will get back $10.50, but the bank has collected $11 from the construction company. When you add up both transactions, you realize the bank has made $.50 for its expenses and profit.

Why does a bank charge interest, but a friend doesn't? A bank is in business to make money. A friend is not looking for a profit when he lends money—although he does expect to be repaid.

Would it be possible for me to take out a loan? Probably not. The law doesn't allow banks to lend money to children. But they wouldn't anyway, because they only lend money to people or groups they consider "good risks." The bank must feel confident that the person will repay the loan. Most kids don't have what the bank is looking for:

1. A good job and a history of paying bills promptly.
2. Property—in case a person can't repay the loan and the bank has to take back the property so it can get its money back.

How does a checking account work? It's a way to keep your money in a safe place while still being able to use it any time you want.

A check is merely a paper slip that you fill out and give to someone. In effect, it tells the bank to take the amount you write on the check out of your account and pay it to the person the check is made out to. When the person gets the check—let's say it's for $75—she will take it to the bank and cash it. The bank gives her real money, $75 in bills, for the check. The cashing of a check begins a process that will result in $75 being withdrawn from your bank to cover the check.

What do people mean when they say "the check bounced"? Suppose a person writes a check for more money than he has in his account. When the person to whom the check is written tries to cash that check, the bank won't give her the money. The check is returned to the person who wrote it (bounced back) and that person is usually charged with a penalty fee. The bank assumes that the check writer should know if he has enough money in his account to cover the check. If a person bounces checks on purpose, knowing he doesn't have enough money in his account, he's committing a crime.

What do you mean when you say "I have to send in the mortgage"? A mortgage is a special loan given by a bank or another lending institution usually to help someone buy a home. The person is expected to pay off the loan (with interest) on a regular basis—usually every month—and does so by sending a check through the mail. That's probably why you hear "I have to send in the mortgage [payment]" so frequently.

How does a credit card work? When you use a credit card to buy something, you're really borrowing money that must be repaid. At the end of the month, you pay the credit card company, which, in turn, pays off the merchants from whom you've bought things. If you don't pay your whole bill to the credit card company within a certain time, you're charged a lot of interest on the balance you haven't repaid.

ABOUT TAXES

Why do we pay taxes? Because we have to pay the government for the community, state and national services it provides. What are a few? Schools, roads, the armed forces, police forces and fire departments.

How does income tax work? Income tax is based on the amount of money you earn during the year. Earnings aren't only what people get from their jobs—although that certainly makes up most of it. Earnings can also include interest on savings accounts, business profits and profits from investments. The way our tax system is supposed to work, the more people earn, the more they pay in income tax.

Take me, for example. I earn a salary. A certain amount of money is withheld each paycheck and sent to the government as part of my income tax. Everybody has a different amount withheld. It depends mainly on a person's income and how many people depend on the worker for support.

By April 15 of each year, almost everyone is required to file a tax return for the year before. We figure out how much in taxes we owe to the city, state and federal governments. If the amount is the same as the amount withheld, we don't owe the government anything. If the amount is more than what was withheld from salary, then we must pay the government the difference. If it is less, the government pays us refund.

THE ULTIMATE QUESTION

Why do parents say "no" to buying us things? (Consider yourself lucky if your child asks this one. What a wonderful springboard for a values discussion!) Several reasons:

1. They can't afford it. Sometimes parents don't have enough money to pay for all the necessities (food, the house, clothing, schooling) *and* for some of the things children want but don't need.
2. They don't think what the child wants is a good buy. As more experienced consumers, parents may think a child can get a better price or find superior quality elsewhere.
3. The item may be unsafe. Parents have a responsibility to try to keep their children from harm.

4. They're philosophically against the purchase. A parent who hates violence, for example, might deny a child a toy gun. A parent committed to a healthy lifestyle may say "no" to a double fudge ice cream cone.

5. A child may ask for too many things. Parents may say "no" even if they have the money and if the item is well-made and not distasteful on moral or philosophical grounds. A parent may say "no" simply because a child is asking for too much. We may feel it's important for you to learn that you can't always have what you want when you want it.

Conclusion

Do Your Best

No parent has yet "gotten it all right." And of seasoned parents, is there one among us who

- has not shoved a candy bar into our toddler's hand simply to keep her quiet so we can swing through the supermarket quickly? (Forget about making the supermarket a learning experience in consumerism.)
- advanced our child's allowance? (Even though the reasons for the advance were wobbly at best.)
- bribed a kid to clean his room? (Grandma's coming in half an hour and will faint if she sees the mounds of clothes on the floor.)
- told a child "I'll think about it." (With the hope she'll forget what she asked for so we don't have to face her tantrum when we say "no.")
- pulled a kid out of a financial jam? (Even though we know it would be a good learning experience if he didn't have money for the rest of the week.)
- directed a child to save money for a rainy day. (Without telling her what that means . . . without being certain why we're even repeating that generation-worn phrase.)
- overspent on an item and gotten into financial hot water? (Thus serving as a rotten role model for well-thought-out money management.)

Parenting isn't easy; but it isn't as difficult as many books, this one included, make it out to be. Stilted parenting, where you think about the consequences of each word you speak and each action you take, is what people do before they have children. Having read every book on the art of parenting, they are either devotees to a particular theory or at sea over how they are going to handle this overwhelming responsibility.

Once you have children, you're rushed for time. How do you teach your child money management or values when you're dashing out the door to work and your daughter casually, and sweetly, asks for $10? "I've agreed to lead a student drive to collect money for the homeless shelter," she says. Do you tell her *your* $10 is not "student money," that she should be saving her own money? Probably not. The cause sounds noble and . . . what the heck? You dig in to your pocket, hand her the money and rush to get to the office on time.

So let's be practical. If you have a general idea of what you want to get across to children, what money means to you, how it can be symbolic of the family values and how to use money in a way that will further those values, then you'll handle tricky parenting situations effectively. Our goal in writing this book is to help you get in touch with those values and to think about how you're conveying them to your children.

Appendix I

Parent Helpers: Books

Great Books for Children

Books do all these:

- Comfort
- Inspire
- Guide
- Bolster
- Influence
- Amuse
- Provide new ideas
- Counsel
- Motivate
- Challenge

Reading (or in the case of younger children, listening to) stories does influence a child's behavior. Below are some wonderful children's books dealing with money and values. A few of these books may be out of print, but you may be able to find them at your local library.

BOOKS DEALING WITH MAKING, SAVING AND SPENDING MONEY

For Younger Readers (Ages Six-Nine) to Read or Be Read To

Leo and Emily's Zoo by Franz Brandenberg and illustrated by Yossi Abolafia. Greenwillow, 1988.

Leo and Emily set up their own zoo and charge admission. Problems occur and all seems lost until their families pitch in.

Arthur's Pet Business by Marc Brown. Little, Brown, 1990.

Arthur wants a pet but must first convince his parents he'll be responsible for it. To do that, he starts a business caring for his neighbor's pets.

Jerome the Babysitter by Eileen Christelow. Clarion, 1985.

The nine Gatorman kids play tricks on Jerome during his first babysitter job. Despite the problems, Jerome surprises himself by managing to get them all to bed. (A picture book.)

A Job for Penny Archer by Ellen Conford and illustrated by Diane Palmisciano. Little, Brown, 1988.
Nine-year-old Jenny wants to buy Mom a fur coat for her birthday, but only has $.27. Jenny tries many money-making schemes and although she can't buy Mom the coat, she finds the perfect gift in a most unlikely place.

The Cinnamon Hen's Autumn Day by Sandra Dutton. Atheneum, 1988.
Is it more fun to rake your own leaves or have Mr. Rabbit's professional lawn service do it for you? (A picture book.)

Ben Goes Into Business by Marilyn Hirsch. Holiday House, 1973.
A young immigrant boy in the early 1900s makes $.60 with a ten-cent investment at Brooklyn's Coney Island. Beautifully illustrated by the author.

Bea and Mr. Jones by Amy Schwarz. Bradbury, 1982.
Five-year-old Bea takes her father's place at work and Mr. Jones, her father, takes her place in kindergarten. He becomes an outstanding kindergartner and the teacher's pet and she comes up with the perfect jingle for the ad agency. (A picture book.)

Alexander, Who Used to Be Rich Last Sunday by Judith Viorst and illustrated by Ray Cruz. Antheneum, 1978.
Alexander was "rich" after his grandparents gave him a dollar. He wanted to save it for a walkie-talkie, but bubble gum, a marble and other temptations slowly deplete his "fortune."

For Upper Elementary School Readers (Ages Ten-Twelve)

Gopher, Tanker and the Admiral by Shirley Climo and illustrated by Eileen McKeating. Crowell, 1984.
Gopher wants to earn money for a bike and together with Tanker, his dog, babysits for Admiral, a cantankerous old neighbor with a broken leg. Gopher gets to like the old man and together they solve a neighborhood mystery.

Mall Mania by Betsy Haynes. Bantam Skylark, 1991.
Beth borrows a friend's credit card and goes on a spree at the mall. She gets deeply into debt and must figure a way out.

The Toothpaste Millionaire by Jean Merrill and illustrated by Jan Palmer. Houghton Mifflin, 1972.

Rufus, upset that toothpaste cost $.79 a tube, makes his own for $.02 a tube. He starts selling it for $.03 and profits grow. With help from friends, his enterprise turns into something fantastic. This book deals with consumerism, entrepreneurship and sharing and caring.

Kid Power by Susan Beth Pfeffer. Watts, 1977.
Janice develops a summer business by doing odd jobs. When she has more jobs than she can handle, she hires other kids to work for her. Business, family relationships and friendships are interwoven in this tale of an enterprising young girl.

Kid Power Strikes Back by Susan Beth Pfeffer. Watts, 1984.
Janice's summer business, Kid Power, ends when school starts. However she misses the business and the money and starts a winter snow shoveling enterprise. She runs into some strong-arm competitors.

How to Get Fabulously Rich by Thomas Rockwell. Franklin Watts, 1990.
Billy wins the lottery. Suddenly everyone he knows feels deservant of a share of the winnings. Was winning worth it?

Blue Denim Blues by Anne W. Smith. Atheneum, 1983.
Shy Janet is good with children and gets a job as an assistant nursery school teacher. In the process, she learns about child abuse and overcomes her shyness.

Oliver Dibbs to the Rescue by Barbara Steiner and illustrated by Eileen Christelow. Four Winds, 1985.
Oliver, his brother Bo, and dog Dolby find ingenious ways to raise money to save endangered animal species.

For Older Readers (Age Thirteen and Up)

Discovered! by Yvonne Green. Bantam, 1988.
At first Kelly is not interested in modeling. Then, as a result of an accident, she is catapulted into this dizzying world. It's fun, but it has its trade-offs.

Shadow in the North by Philip Pullman. Knopf, 1988.
Sally's investment counseling business causes a client to lose money. When Sally tries to find out why, she gets drawn into a complex plot that involves murder, the London theatre and spiritualism.

It Happened at Cecelia's by Erika Tamar. Atheneum, 1989.
Andy's father is half-owner of Cecelia's, a Hungarian restaurant

in Manhattan's Greenwich Village. Trouble brews when the mob tries to take it over.

Seventeen Against the Dealer by Cynthia Voigt. Atheneum, 1989.
In the last story of the Tillermans, Dicey invests her money in her own shop, which stores and does maintenance work on boats. When she tries to make her own boat, she runs up against problems she never expected.

BOOKS DEALING WITH FAMILIES FACING MONEY PROBLEMS

Tybee Trimble's Hard Times by Lila Perl. Clarion, 1984.
Tybee's father is quitting his job to study for the bar exam, so there's no money for frills or extras, such as tickets to the circus. Even if she makes enough money for a ticket, she faces the dilemma of whether to go by herself and leave the rest of the family behind. (Ages nine-twelve)

First Things First by Kristi D. Holl. Atheneum, 1986.
Shelly's parents can't afford the increased cost of camp this year. To fill in the summer months, she resells items bought at garage sales. As profitable as this is, Shelly "overdoes" her work and finds she is missing out on other important things in her life. (Ages ten-thirteen)

Credit-Card Carole by Sheila Solomon Klass. Scribner's, 1987.
Carole's dad, a successful dentist, gives up his profession to return to acting. Family income goes down and Carole, whose first love is shopping, runs up an enormous credit-card debt. Problems in her friends' lives help her view her own situation in a new light. (Ages twelve-fourteen)

BOOKS DEALING WITH SHARING, CARING AND GIVING

The Gold Coin by Alma F. Ada. Atheneum, 1991.
A picture book based on a Spanish folktale about Juan, a thief, who hears of Dona Josefa's gold coin and sets out to steal it. As he travels to find her, he meets farmers and villagers who need his help with their chores. By the time he finds Dona Josefa, he has found another type of treasure—a human one. (Ages five-eight)

No Time for Christmas by Judy Delton and illustrated by Anastasia Mitchell. Carolrhoda, 1988.
Brimhall and Bear, two animal-character cousins, secretly and separately decide to take jobs to buy each other Christmas pres-

ents. One works nights, the other days, so they hardly see each other anymore. (Ages six-eight)

Brothers by Florence B. Freedman and illustrated by Robert Andrew Parker. Harper and Row, 1985.
In a story based on an old Hebrew legend, two brothers inherit their father's land and split it equally. Their father's wishes that they always be friends and help each other cause them to do something special for one another. Beautifully illustrated. (Ages five-nine)

The Giving Tree by Shel Silverstein. Harper and Row, 1964.
A parable for all ages, this is a sensitive tale of giving (and taking) until there is no more to give . . . or so it seems. Best to read to younger children (five-seven); eight-year-olds and older can read it independently.

Jefferson by Mary Frances Shura and illustrated by Susan Swan. Dodd, 1984.
Jefferson's family can't afford to give him a birthday party, so the neighborhood kids decide to work and earn money for a party in honor on the last day of school. The problems they faced never overshadowed their goal. (Ages nine-twelve)

The Gift of the Magi by O. Henry was originally published by Doubleday in 1906 but can now be found in almost any collection of O. Henry short stories. This classic tale of love, giving and sacrifice delights children when it's read to them (ages six through twelve) or when they read it themselves.

TALES OF TREASURE AND WEALTH

The Treasure by Uri Shulevitz. McGraw-Hill Ryerson, 1978.
This parable is based on an old Hebrew folktale. Isaac, following a voice in his dream, goes to the capital city to look for a treasure under the bridge by the royal palace. There is nothing there; instead he finds the treasure back in his own home. Read to children ages five through eight; nine and older probably can read it independently.

King Midas by Nathaniel Hawthorne and illustrated by Paul Galdone. McGraw Hill, 1959.
Based on the Greek legend of King Midas, the greedy king who wished that everything he touched would turn to gold. He got his wish but, of course, found out that some things were more precious than gold. Can be read to seven- through nine-year-

olds; ten and up might be ready to read it independently.

All the Money in the World by Bill Brittain and illustrated by Charles Robinson. HarperCollins, 1979.

A boy catches a leprechaun and gets his wish—all the money in the world. At first he's delighted as he looks at the huge pile of money stacked in his backyard. Then the problems and the trouble begin. (Ages eleven-fourteen)

Jason and the Money Tree by Sonia Levitan and illustrated by Pat Grant Porter. Harcourt Brace, 1974.

Jason plants a crumpled $10 bill and really grows a money tree. But complications arise that teach Jason some important lessons about life. (Ages eleven-fourteen)

BOOKS THAT HELP KIDS MAKE CHOICES—"PLOT YOUR OWN STORY" BOOKS

Hide and Snake by Keith Baker, Harcourt Brace, 1991.

A brightly colored snake plays a game of hide and seek with the reader. (Ages five-eight)

You Can Make a Difference: The Story of Martin Luther King, Jr. by Anne Bailey. Bantam Skylark Books, 1990.

The reader plots his own story using the events of this extraordinary civil rights leader's life. (Ages seven-twelve)

Your Very Own Robot by R.A. Montgomery. Bantam Skylark Books, 1982.

The reader has fun with her very own robot. The adventures depend on the choices she makes. (Ages seven-nine)

You Are Invisible by Susan Saunders. Bantam Skylark Books, 1989.

The reader moves into an old house and discovers a cloak of invisibility. (Ages seven-twelve)

The Case of the Silk King by Shannon Gilligan. Bantam Books, 1986.

The reader is a detective who receives an envelope with two $1,000 bills, a plane ticket to Thailand, and a newspaper article about the disappearance of Jim Thompson, an ex-U.S. spy during World War II who started a successful silk business in Thailand after the war. To find the Silk King, you must plot your own story. (Ages eight-twelve)

Dream Trips by R.A. Montgomery, Bantam Skylark Books, 1983.

Readers have adventures with a lion, in a hot air balloon, or on a flying horse—depending upon their choices. (Ages eight-twelve)

The Circus by Edward Packard, Bantam Skylark Books, 1981.
The reader is the star of the circus, making decisions about what act he wants to perform and what adventures he wants to have. (Ages eight-twelve)

Sugarcane Island by Edward Packard. Bantam Books, 1986.
A shipwreck starts the adventure and the rest is up to the choices made by the reader. (Ages nine-thirteen)

Bully on the Bus by Carl W. Bosch. Parenting Press, 1988.
The reader has to make decisions and choices surrounding how to deal with a bully. (Ages ten-thirteen)

Finders, Keepers? by Elizabeth Crary. Parenting Press, 1987.
What are the choices and what are the consequences when one finds lost property? (Ages ten-thirteen)

Appendix II

Parent Helpers: Computer Software

Bits and Bytes to Help Young Entrepreneurs and Money Managers

The computer age gives kids a terrific opportunity to hone their math and money skills. Below are some of the best and most reasonably priced programs on the market today.

The Little Shoppers Kit (Ages six-nine)
Objectives include practice in:

- basic math skills
- money recognition
- making change
- decision making

Special features: Played with a group of children who have different roles, such as store manager, cashier, bagger and customer. Comes with toy money and simulated supermarket products.
Company: Tom Snyder Productions in Cambridge, Massachusetts
Telephone: 800-342-0236
For use with: Apple computers

Math Shop Jr. (Ages six-nine) and **Math Shop** (Ages nine-fourteen)
Math Shop Jr. objectives include practice in:

- basic math functions with whole numbers
- indentifying values of coins

Math Shop deals with advanced concepts that include working with percentages, ratios and proportions.
Company: Scholastic, Inc., in Jefferson City, Missouri
Telephone: 800-541-5513
For use with: Apple II Plus, IIe, IIc, II G.S, and a special version for the Macintosh

Money! Money! (Ages seven-nine)
Objective is to develop skills in:
- counting money
- determining if there's enough money to buy something
- counting change

Company: Hartley Courseware, Inc., in Dimondale, Michigan
Telephone: 800-247-1380
For use with: Apple II series or Franklin ACE 1000

Math for the Young Consumer (Ages nine-fourteen)
Objectives include proficiency in:
- earning and saving money
- shopping at the supermarket and during sale times
- managing your money

Company: Orange Cherry Software in Pound Ridge, New York
Telephone: 800-672-6002
For use with: TRS-80, IBM-PC, Apple II series, and Commodore 64 (only on a 5¼″ disk)

Be a Smart Shopper (Ages eleven-fourteen)
Objectives are to:
- work within a budget and differentiate needs and wants
- interpret advertising claims
- do comparison shopping

Company: Victoria Learning Systems in Fairfield, Connecticut
Telephone: 800-232-2224
For use with: Apple II series or TRS-80 (only on 5¼″ disks)

The Whatsit Corporation: Survival Math Skills (Ages eleven and up)
Objective is to simulate a real business so a youngster can run a small one-product business for a simulated period of six months—with all the challenges of a real business:
- hiring and firing
- paying taxes
- borrowing money and setting prices

Company: Wings for Learning-Sunburst in Scott's Valley, California
Telephone: 800-321-7511
For use with: Apple II series, Commodore 64 (only on 5¼″ disk), IBM PC and PC Jr.

BIBLIOGRAPHY

Books

Ames, Louise Bates. *Questions Parents Ask*. Doubleday, 1990.

Ames, Louise Bates and Carol Chase Haber. *Your Eight-Year-Old*. Delacorte, 1989.

Borneman, Earnest. *The Psychoanalysis of Money*. Urizen Books, Inc., 1976.

Cantwell, Lois. *Money and Banking*. Franklin Watts, 1984.

Clabby, John F. and Maurice J. Elias. *Teach Your Child Decision Making: An Effective 8-Step Program for Parents to Teach Children of All Ages to Solve Everyday Problems and Make Sound Decisions*. Doubleday, 1987.

Crook de Camp, Catherine. *Teach Your Child to Manage Money*. U.S. News and World Reports Books, 1974.

Estess, Patricia Schiff. *Remarriage and Your Money*. Little, Brown, 1992.

Feiden, Karyn. *Parents' Guide to Raising Responsible Kids: Preschool Through the Teen Years*. Prentice Hall, 1991.

Fodor, R.V. *Nickels, Dimes, and Dollars: How Currency Works*. William Morrow, 1980.

Kyte, Kathy S. *The Kids' Complete Guide to Money*. Alfred A. Knopf, 1984.

McNeal, James U. *Kids as Cosumers: A Handbook of Marketing to Children*. Free Press, 1992.

Salk, Lee. *The Complete Dr. Salk*. New American Library, 1983.

Schaeffer, Charles E. *How to Talk to Children About Really Important Things*. HarperCollins, 1984.

Scharlatt, Elisabeth L. *Kids: Day in and Day Out*. Simon and Schuster, 1979.

Shiff, Eileen. *Experts Advise Parents: A Guide to Raising Loving, Responsible Children*. Delacorte, 1990.

Spock, Benjamin and Michael B. Rothenberg. *Dr. Spock's Baby and Child Care*. Pocket Books, 1992.

Taffel, Ron. *Parenting by Heart*. Addison-Wesley, 1991.

Weinstein, Grace W., *Children and Money: A Parents' Guide*. Signet, 1985.

Wilkinson, Elizabeth. *Making Cents: Every Kid's Guide to Money*. Little Brown, 1989.

Articles

Arent, Ruth. "To Tell the Truth." *Learning*, 19 (February, 1991): 72.

Comer, James P. "How Not to Spoil Your Child" *Parents*, 67 (March, 1992): 165.

Kutner, Lawrence. "Learning Right From Wrong." *New York Times*, 15 March 1990

Kutner, Lawrence. "Inevitable Envy: Coping With Rivalry and 'Me' Too." *New York Times*, 22 August 1991

Kutner, Lawrence. "Children and the Psychology of Spending Money." *New York Times*, 23 April 1992.

Kutner, Lawrence. "A First Job Can Provide Value Beyond Just Money." *New York Times*, 28 May 1992.

Kutner, Lawrence. "When Children Steal, Parents Should Know Why." *New York Times*, 10 September 1992.

Reissman, Rose. "Consumer Smarts." *Learning* 19 (November-December 1990): 32-33

"Nighmares on Jobs Street." *Zillions* 2 (August-September 1991): 8-10.

"The Allowance Report." *Zillions* 3 (April-May 1993): 8-11.

INDEX

Other Books of Interest

Raising Happy Kids on a Reasonable Budget, by Patricia Gallagher—Budget-stretching, dollar-ing tips on food, clothing, education, entertainment, toys, daycare, grooming, and more. *#70184/ pages/$10.95, paperback*

Confessions of a Happily Organized Family, by Deniece Schofield—Shows how to work as a fa to establish a comfortable sense of order to your home. *#1145/246 pages/$10.95, paperback*

Step-by-Step Parenting: A Guide to Successful Living with a Blended Family—Offers advice inspiration on everything from the games children sometimes play, rights of the stepparent, n changes, and the advantages and disadvantages of adoption. *#70202/224 pages/$11.99, paperbac*

Families Writing—More than 50 writing exercises show you how to build a close-knit family as learn how to capture life's precious moments on paper—before they slip away. *#10294/198 pa $12.95, paperback*

Roots for Kids—You will delight as your child finds a sense of self through learning about y family's history. This one-of-a-kind guide shows you how to spark your child's interest in geneal *#70093/128 pages/$7.95, paperback*

Roughing it Easy—Have fun in the great outdoors with these ingenious tips! You'll learn w equipment to take, how to plan, set up a campsite, build a fire, backpack—even how to camp du winter. *#70260/256 pages/$14.99 paperback*

You Can Find More Time for Yourself Every Day—Professionals, working mothers, college dents—if you're in a hurry, you need this time-saving guide! Quizzes, tests, and charts will show how to make the most of your minutes! *#70258/208 pages/$12.99 paperback*

The Organization Map, by Pam McClellan—This upbeat, lighthearted book offers an easily follo roadmap to simpler, less cluttered living. *#70224/208 pages/$12.95, paperback*

How to Get Organized When You Don't Have the Time, by Stephanie Culp—Combines time-mana ment principles with specific, workable ideas for organizing key trouble areas (including clos garage, and paperwork). *#1354/216 pages/$10.99, paperback*

Is There Life After Housework?—All you need to take the dread out of housework are some ingeni ideas and a little inspiration—find them both in this bestseller! *#10292/216 pages/$10.99, paperb*

Clutter's Last Stand—You think you're organized, yet closets bulge around you. Get out of clu denial with loads of practical advice. *#1122/280 pages/$10.95, paperback*

A Parent's Guide to Band and Orchestra, by Jim Probasco—Includes the most often asked questi by parents during Probasco's seventeen years as a public school music teacher. *#70075/136 pa $7.95, paperback*

A Parent's Guide to Teaching Music, by Jim Probasco—Even if you have no musical training, book shows you how to teach a child the basics of reading music, and get them started playing instrument. #70082/136 pages/$7.95, paperback

Write to the address below for a FREE catalog of all Betterway Books. To order books directly from the publisher, include $3.00 postage and handling for one book, $1.00 for each additional book. Ohio residents add 5½% sales tax. Allow 30 days for delivery.

Betterway Books
1507 Dana Avenue
Cincinnati, Ohio 45207

VISA/MasterCard orders call TOLL-FREE
1-800-289-0963

Prices subject to change without notice. Stock may be limited on some books. 3131